CONTENTS

D1239991

INTERACTIVE

Read-Aloud

ANTHOLOGY with PLAYS

Grade 5

Macmillan
McGraw-Hill

ACKNOWLEDGMENTS

"La Bamba" from BASEBALL IN APRIL by Gary Soto. Copyright © 1990 by Gary Soto. Used by permission of Harcourt Brace Jovanovich, Inc.

"Sally Ann Thunder Ann Whirlwind" from AMERICAN TALL TALES by Mary Pope Osborne. Copyright © 1991 by Mary Pope Osborne. Used by permission of Alfred A. Knopf, Inc.

"A Symphony of Trees" by Charles Ghigna from *Children's Digest*, July/August 2004. Copyright © 2004 by Children's Better Health Institute, Benjamin Franklin Literary & Medical Society, Inc. Used by permission of Children's Better Health Institute, Benjamin Franklin Literary & Medical Society, Inc.

"Who's There?" from THE NINE BILLION NAMES OF GOD by Arthur C. Clarke. Copyright © 1958 by United Newspapers Magazine Corporation. Used by permission of Harcourt Brace Jovanovich, Inc.

"Barry: The Dog Who Saved People" by Margaret Davidson from GIVE A DOG A BONE: STORIES, POEMS, JOKES, AND RIDDLES ABOUT DOGS compiled by Joanna Cole and Stephanie Calmenson. Copyright © 1996 by Joanna Cole and Stephanie Calmenson. Used by permission of Scholastic Inc.

"Close Encounters of the Bear Kind" by Susan Quinlan from *Muse*, November 2000. Copyright © 2000 by Carus Publishing Company. Used by permission of Carus Publishing Company.

"Snakebite" from RATTLESNAKE DANCE: TRUE TALES, MYSTERIES AND RATTLESNAKE CEREMONIES by Jennifer Owings Dewey. Copyright © 1997 by Jennifer Owings Dewey. Used by permission of Caroline House.

Excerpt from ON THE MALL IN WASHINGTON, D.C.: A VISIT TO AMERICA'S FRONT YARD by Brent Ashabranner. Copyright © 2002 by Brent Ashabranner. Used by permission of Twenty-First Century Books.

"Tradition" from UNDER THE SUNDAY TREE by Eloise Greenfield. Copyright © 1988 by Eloise Greenfield. Used by permission of Harper Trophy, a Division of HarperCollins Publishers.

Excerpt from BORN TO BE A COWGIRL: A SPIRITED RIDE THROUGH THE OLD WEST by Candace Savage. Copyright © 2001 by Candace Savage. Used by permission of Tricycle Press.

"Deborah Sampson: Patriot Soldier Disguised as a Man" from HEROINES OF THE AMERICAN REVOLUTION by Diane Silcox-Jarrett. Copyright © 1998 by Green Angel Press. Used by permission of Green Angel Press.

"Motivating Kids: A Visit with *Kids Voting USA*" by Meg Chorlian from *Cobblestone*, March 2004. Copyright © 2004 by Carus Publishing Company. Used by permission of Carus Publishing Company.

Excerpt from DEAR WORLD: HOW CHILDREN AROUND THE WORLD FEEL ABOUT OUR ENVIRONMENT, edited by Lannis Temple. Copyright © 1993 by Random House, Inc. Used by permission of Random House, Inc.

Continued on page 242

A

The *McGraw·Hill* Companies

Macmillan
McGraw-Hill

Published by Macmillan/McGraw-Hill, of McGraw-Hill Education, a division of The McGraw-Hill Companies, Inc., Two Penn Plaza, New York, New York 10121.

Printed in the United States of America

1 2 3 4 5 6 7 8 9 10 005 11 10 09 08 07 06 05

INTERACTIVE
Read-Aloud
ANTHOLOGY with PLAYS

～ Developing Listening Comprehension ～

Read Alouds help to build students' listening comprehension. This anthology offers selections from a variety of genres, including biography, fiction, folk tales, nonfiction, primary sources, songs, and poetry, to share with students. Instruction is provided with each selection to develop specific **comprehension strategies.** Students are asked to **set a purpose for listening,** as well as to **determine the author's purpose** for writing. Using the instruction provided, each Read Aloud becomes an enjoyable, purposeful learning experience.

～ What Makes a Read Aloud Interactive? ～

With each selection, **Teacher Think Alouds** are provided to help you model the use of comprehension strategies during reading. Using Think Alouds allows students to listen and to observe how a good reader uses strategies to get meaning from text. After reading, students are given the opportunity to apply the comprehension strategy. Students are asked to "think aloud" as they apply the strategy. By listening to a **Student Think Aloud** you can determine if the student is applying the comprehension strategy appropriately and with understanding.

Think-Aloud Copying Masters included in the Read-Aloud Anthology provide sentence starters to help students "think aloud" about a strategy.

Plays and Choral Readings

Reader's Theater for Building Fluency

You can use the plays and choral readings found at the back of this anthology to perform a Reader's Theater with students. Reading fluency is developed by repeated practice in reading text, especially when the reading is done orally. Reader's Theater can help build students' fluency skills because it engages them in a highly motivating activity that provides an opportunity to read— and reread—text orally. As students practice their assigned sections of the "script," they have multiple opportunities to increase their accuracy in word recognition and their rate of reading. Students are also strongly motivated to practice reading with appropriate phrasing and expression.

Performing Reader's Theater

• Assign speaking roles.

• Do not always assign the speaking role with the most text to the most fluent reader. Readers who need practice reading need ample opportunity to read.

• Have students rehearse by reading and rereading their lines over several days. In these rehearsals, allow time for teacher and peer feedback about pace, phrasing, and expression.

• Students do not memorize their lines, but rather read their lines from the script.

• No sets, costumes, or props are necessary.

LA BAMBA

from *Baseball in April*
by Gary Soto

Genre: Realistic Fiction

Text Structure: Description

Comprehension Strategy: Analyze Story Structure

Think-Aloud Copying Master number 5

Before Reading

Genre: Explain to students that you will be reading aloud a work of realistic fiction about what happens when a boy volunteers for a school talent show. Point out that realistic fiction combines fictional characters with events that could happen in real life.

Expand Vocabulary: To add to students' understanding of the story, introduce the following words:

> *volunteered:* offered to do something
>
> *limelight:* the focus of attention
>
> *applause:* clapping
>
> *pantomime:* a silent performance
>
> *rehearsal:* a practice session for a performance

Set a Purpose for Reading: Direct students to listen for details that place the main character in a modern setting, yet show that he went to school in the recent past. Have them read to find out why the story is called "La Bamba."

During Reading

Use the Think Alouds during the first reading of the story. Notes about the genre and cultural perspectives may be used during subsequent readings.

LA BAMBA

by Gary Soto

Manuel was the fourth of seven children and looked like a lot of kids in his neighborhood: black hair, brown face, and skinny legs scuffed from summer play. But summer was giving way to fall: the trees were turning red, the lawns brown, and the pomegranate trees were heavy with fruit. Manuel walked to school in the frosty morning, kicking leaves and thinking of tomorrow's talent show.[1] He was still amazed that he had volunteered. He was going to pretend to sing Ritchie Valens's "La Bamba" before the entire school.

Why did I raise my hand? he asked himself, but in his heart he knew the answer. He yearned for the limelight. He wanted applause as loud as a thunderstorm, and to hear his friends say, "Man, that was bad!" And he wanted to impress the girls, especially Petra Lopez, the second-prettiest girl in his class. The prettiest was already taken by his friend Ernie. Manuel knew he should be reasonable, since he himself was not great-looking, just average.

Manuel kicked through the fresh-fallen leaves. When he got to school he realized he had forgotten his math workbook. If his teacher found out, he would have to stay after school and miss practice for the talent show. But fortunately for him, they did drills that morning.

During lunch Manuel hung around with Benny, who was also in the talent show. Benny was going to play the trumpet in spite of the fat lip he had gotten playing football.

"How do I look?" Manuel asked. He cleared his throat and started moving his lips in pantomime. No words came out, just a hiss that sounded like a snake. Manuel tried to look emotional, flailing his arms on the high notes and opening his eyes and mouth as wide as he could when he came to "*Para bailar la baaaaammmba.*"

After Manuel finished, Benny said it looked all right, but suggested Manuel dance while he sang. Manuel thought for a moment and decided it was a good idea.

"Yeah, just think you're like Michael Jackson or someone like that," Benny suggested. "But don't get carried away."

During rehearsal, Mr. Roybal, nervous about his debut as the school's talent coordinator, cursed under his breath when the lever that controlled the speed of the record player jammed.

"Darn," he growled, trying to force the lever. "What's wrong with you?"

"Is it broken?" Manuel asked, bending over for a closer look. It looked all right to him.

Mr. Roybal assured Manuel that he would have a good record player at the talent show, even if it meant bringing his own stereo from home.

Manuel sat in a folding chair, twirling his record on his thumb. He watched a skit about personal hygiene, a mother-and-daughter violin duo, five first-grade girls jumping rope, a karate kid breaking boards, and a skit about the pilgrims. If the record player hadn't been broken, he would have gone after the karate kid, an easy act to follow, he told himself.[2]

As he twirled his forty-five record, Manuel thought they had a great talent show. The entire school would be amazed. His mother and father would be proud, and his brothers and sisters would be jealous and pout. It would be a night to remember.

Benny walked onto the stage, raised his trumpet to his mouth, and waited for his cue. Mr. Roybal raised his hand like a symphony conductor and let it fall dramatically. Benny inhaled and blew so loud that Manuel dropped his record, which rolled across the cafeteria floor until it hit a wall. Manuel raced after it, picked it up, and wiped it clean.

"Boy, I'm glad it didn't break," he said with a sigh.

That night Manuel had to do the dishes and a lot of homework, so he could only practice in the shower. In bed he prayed that he wouldn't mess up. He prayed that it wouldn't be like when he was a first-grader. For Science Week he had wired together a C battery and a bulb, and told everyone he had discovered how a flashlight worked. He was so pleased with himself that he practiced for hours pressing the wire to the battery, making the bulb wink a dim, orangish light. He showed it to so many kids in his neighborhood that when it was time to show his class how a flashlight worked, the battery was dead. He pressed the wire to the battery, but the bulb didn't respond. He pressed until his thumb hurt and some kids in the back started snickering.

But Manuel fell asleep confident that nothing would go wrong this time.

Think Aloud

[2] *The writer uses details that show the story's setting is modern but not as modern as today. Manuel uses a record, while today a student might have a CD. Mr. Roybal uses a record player. Otherwise, Manuel's school sounds a lot like our own.*

The next morning his father and mother beamed at him. They were proud that he was going to be in the talent show.

"I wish you would tell us what you're doing," his mother said. His father, a pharmacist who wore a blue smock with his name on a plastic rectangle, looked up from the newspaper and sided with his wife. "Yes, what are you doing in the talent show?"

"You'll see," Manuel said with his mouth full of Cheerios.

The day whizzed by, and so did his afternoon chores and dinner. Suddenly he was dressed in his best clothes and standing next to Benny backstage, listening to the commotion as the cafeteria filled with school kids and parents. The lights dimmed, and Mr. Roybal, sweaty in a tight suit and a necktie with a large knot, wet his lips and parted the stage curtains.

"Good evening, everyone," the kids behind the curtain heard him say. "Good evening to you," some of the smart-alecky kids said back to him.

"Tonight we bring you the best John Burroughs Elementary has to offer, and I'm sure that you'll be both pleased and amazed that our little school houses so much talent. And now, without further ado, let's get on with the show." He turned and, with a swish of his hand, commanded, "Part the curtain." The curtains parted in jerks. A girl dressed as a toothbrush and a boy dressed as a dirty gray tooth walked onto the stage and sang:

> Brush, brush, brush
> Floss, floss, floss
> Gargle the germs away—hey! hey! hey!

After they finished singing, they turned to Mr. Roybal, who dropped his hand. The toothbrush dashed around the stage after the dirty tooth, which was laughing and having a great time until it slipped and nearly rolled off the stage.

Mr. Roybal jumped out and caught it just in time. "Are you OK?"

The dirty tooth answered, "Ask my dentist," which drew laughter and applause from the audience.

The violin duo played next, and except for one time when the girl got lost, they sounded fine. People applauded, and some even stood up. Then the first-grade girls maneuvered onto the stage while jumping rope. They were all smiles and bouncing ponytails as a hundred cameras flashed at once. Mothers "aahed" and fathers sat up proudly.

The karate kid was next. He did a few kicks, yells, and chops, and finally, when his father held up a board, punched it in two. The audience clapped and looked at each other, wide-eyed with respect. The boy bowed to the audience, and father and son ran off the stage.

Manuel remained behind the stage shivering with fear. He mouthed the words to "La Bamba" and swayed from left to right. Why did he raise his hand and volunteer? Why couldn't he have just sat there like the rest of the kids and not said anything? While the karate kid was on stage, Mr. Roybal, more sweaty than before, took Manuel's forty-five record and placed it on the new record player.

"You ready?" Mr. Roybal asked.

"Yeah . . . ."

Mr. Roybal walked back on stage and announced that Manuel Gomez, a fifth-grader in Mrs. Knight's class, was going to pantomime Ritchie Valens's classic hit "La Bamba."

The cafeteria roared with applause. Manuel was nervous but loved the noisy crowd. He pictured his mother and father applauding loudly and his brothers and sisters also clapping, though not as energetically.

Manuel walked on stage and the song started immediately. Glassy-eyed from the shock of being in front of so many people, Manuel moved his lips and swayed in a made-up dance step. He couldn't see his parents, but he could see his brother Mario, who was a year younger, thumb-wrestling with a friend. Mario was wearing Manuel's favorite shirt—, he would deal with Mario later. He saw some other kids get up and head for the drinking fountain, and a baby sitting in the middle of an aisle sucking her thumb and watching him intently.

What am I doing here? thought Manuel. This is no fun at all. Everyone was just sitting there. Some people were moving to the beat, but most were just watching him, like they would a monkey at the zoo.

But when Manuel did a fancy dance step, there was a burst of applause and some girls screamed.[3] Manuel tried another dance step. He heard more applause and screams and started getting into the groove. But the record got stuck, and he had to sing

> Para bailar la bamba
> Para bailar la bamba
> Para bailar la bamba
> Para bailar la bamba

again and again.

Manuel couldn't believe his bad luck. The audience began to laugh and stand up in their chairs. Manuel remembered how the forty-five record had dropped from his hand and rolled across the cafeteria floor. It probably got scratched, he thought, and now it was stuck, and he was stuck dancing and moving his lips to the same words over and over. He had never been so embarrassed. He would have to ask his parents to move the family out of town.

After Mr. Roybal ripped the needle across the record, Manuel slowed his dance steps to a halt. He didn't know what to do except bow to the audience, which applauded wildly, and scoot off the stage, on the verge of tears. This was worse than the homemade flashlight. At least no one laughed then, they just snickered.

Manuel stood alone, trying hard to hold back the tears as Benny, center stage, played his trumpet. Manuel was jealous because he sounded great, then mad as he recalled that it was Benny's loud trumpet playing that made the forty-five record fly out of his hands. But when the entire cast lined up for a curtain call, Manuel received a burst of applause that was so loud it shook the walls of the cafeteria. Later, as he mingled with the kids and parents, everyone patted him on the shoulder and told him, "Way to go. You were really funny."

Funny? Manuel thought. Did he do something funny?

Funny. Crazy. Hilarious. These were the words people said to him. He was confused, but beyond caring. All he knew was that people were paying attention to him, and his brothers and sisters looked at him with a mixture of jealousy and awe. He was going to pull Mario aside and punch him in the arm for wearing his shirt, but he cooled it. He was enjoying the limelight. A teacher brought him cookies and punch, and the popular kids who had never before given him the time of day now clustered around him. Ricardo, the editor of the school bulletin, asked him how he made the needle stick.

"It just happened," Manuel said, crunching on a star-shaped cookie.

At home that night his father, eager to undo the buttons on his shirt and ease into his recliner, asked Manuel the same thing, how he managed to make the song stick on the words *"Para bailar la bamba."*

Manuel thought quickly and reached for scientific jargon he had read in magazines. "Easy, Dad. I used laser tracking with high optics and low functional decibels per channel." His proud but confused father told him to be quiet and go to bed.

"Ah, *que niños tan truchas,*" he said as he walked to the kitchen for a glass of milk. "I don't know how you kids nowadays get so smart."

Manuel, feeling happy, went to his bedroom, undressed, and slipped into his pajamas. He looked in the mirror and began to pantomime "La Bamba," but stopped because he was tired of the song. He crawled into bed. The sheets were as cold as the moon that stood over the peach tree in their backyard.

He was relieved that the day was over. Next year, when they asked for volunteers for the talent show, he wouldn't raise his hand. Probably.

After Reading

Retell the Story: Ask students to retell the story by acting out a scene where Manuel calls a friend to explain what happened. Have students help each other to remember important details by asking questions.

Student Think Aloud

Use Copying Master number 5 to prompt students to give examples of details that tell about Manuel, the plot, and the setting of the story.

"I noticed the author . . ."

Cultural Perspective

"La Bamba," a pop song that Ritchie Valens recorded in 1958, was based on a classic Mexican folk song about a mariachi dance. The song became popular again in the 1980s, the setting of this story, when a movie was made on the Spanish word *bambolear*, which means "to swing."

Think and Respond

1. How can you tell that people thought Manuel had planned a funny performance? *Possible response: They asked him how he made the needle stick. They thought he'd made it stick on purpose.* **Inferential**

2. How is this story like other realistic fiction you have read, such as "Miss Alaineus"? *Possible response: Realistic fiction tells about realistic people, settings, and situations. Both examples tell about students in school who turn a mistake into a success.* **Genre**

3. What do you think the author wants you to understand by reading this story about Manuel? *Possible response: Even when things go wrong, they can turn out all right.* **Author's Purpose**

Sally Ann Thunder Ann Whirlwind

by Mary Pope Osborne

Genre: Tall Tale

Text Structure: Description

Comprehension Strategy: Analyze Story Structure

Think-Aloud Copying Master number 5

 Before Reading

Genre: Remind students that in a tall tale the characters are larger than life, usually heroes who use amazing powers to solve problems. Point out that many tall tales combine American history during its frontier days and the exaggerated storytelling of ordinary people.

Expand Vocabulary: Introduce the following words and phrases before reading the tall tale:

> *crotch of the tree:* the part of a tree where it forks into two branches
>
> *extraordinary:* very unusual
>
> *varmint:* an unpleasant person or animal
>
> *gizzard:* a stomach

Set a Purpose for Reading: Invite students to listen to the story to identify language and literary devices that are used to develop characters.

 During Reading

Use the Analyze Story Structure comprehension Think Alouds during the first reading of the story. Notes about the genre may be used during subsequent readings. Emphasize the humor and exaggerated details during the read aloud.

Sally Ann Thunder Ann Whirlwind

by Mary Pope Osborne

Notes on the Story

The backwoods women of Tennessee and Kentucky endured the same hardships as the men as they tried to carve a life out of the wilderness. They helped build cabins and clear land for planting. They hauled water from springs, grew cotton for clothes, and hunted wild animals. Though no early tall tales celebrate an abiding heroine, the Davy Crockett Almanacks *do present rugged frontier women in a number of vignettes, such as "Sal Fink, the Mississippi Screamer," "Nance Bowers Taming a Bear," "Katy Goodgrit and the Wolves," and "Sappina Wing and the Crocodile." In these stories the Davy Crockett character tells about comically outrageous women who display amazing boldness and ingenuity.*

In the following tale I have chosen to combine these various female characters into a single heroine—and have called her Sally Ann Thunder Ann Whirlwind, the name of Davy's fictional wife, who is briefly mentioned in the Davy Crockett Almanacks.

One early spring day, when the leaves of the white oaks were about as big as a mouse's ear, Davy Crockett set out alone through the forest to do some bear hunting. Suddenly it started raining real hard, and he felt obliged to stop for shelter under a tree. As he shook the rain out of his coonskin cap, he got sleepy, so he laid back into the crotch of the tree, and pretty soon he was snoring.

Davy slept so hard, he didn't wake up until nearly sundown. And when he did, he discovered that somehow or another in all that sleeping his head had gotten stuck in the crotch of the tree, and he couldn't get it out.

Well, Davy roared loud enough to make the tree lose all its little mouse-ear leaves. He twisted and turned and carried on for over an hour, but still that tree wouldn't let go. Just as he was about to give himself up for a goner, he heard a girl say, "What's the matter, stranger?"

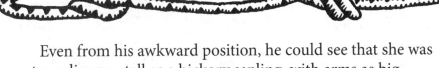

Even from his awkward position, he could see that she was extraordinary—tall as a hickory sapling, with arms as big as a keelboat tiller's.

"My head's stuck, sweetie," he said. "And if you help me get it free, I'll give you a pretty little comb."

"Don't call me sweetie," she said. "And don't worry about giving me no pretty little comb, neither. I'll free your old coconut, but just because I want to."

Then this extraordinary girl did something that made Davy's hair stand on end. She reached in a bag and took out a bunch of rattlesnakes. She tied all the wriggly critters together to make a long rope, and as she tied, she kept talking. "I'm not a shy little colt," she said. "And I'm not a little singing nightingale, neither. I can tote a steamboat on my back, outscream a panther, and jump over my own shadow.**1** I can double up crocodiles any day, and I like to wear a hornets' nest for my Sunday bonnet."

As the girl looped the ends of her snake rope to the top of the branch that was trapping Davy, she kept bragging: "I'm a streak of lightning set up edgeways and buttered with quicksilver. I can outgrin, outsnort, outrun, outlift, outsneeze, outsleep, outlie any varmint from Maine to Louisiana. Furthermore, *sweetie*, I can blow out the moonlight and sing a wolf to sleep." Then she pulled on the other end of the snake rope so hard, it seemed as if she might tear the world apart.

The right-hand fork of that big tree bent just about double. Then Davy slid his head out as easy as you please. For a minute he was so dizzy, he couldn't tell up from down. But when he got everything going straight again, he took a good look at that girl. "What's your name, ma'am?"

"Sally Ann Thunder Ann Whirlwind," she said. "But if you mind your manners, you can call me Sally."

From then on Davy Crockett was crazy in love with Sally Ann Thunder Ann Whirlwind. He asked everyone he knew about her, and everything he heard caused another one of Cupid's arrows to jab him in the gizzard.

"Oh, I know Sally!" the preacher said. "She can dance a rock to pieces and ride a panther bareback!"**2**

"Sally's a good ole friend of mine," the blacksmith said. "Once I seen her crack a walnut with her front teeth."

Think Aloud

1 I notice the author uses many unlikely details in this tall tale, such as when Sally ties rattle-snakes together to make a rope. Another example is when Sally tells Davy Crockett she can tote a steamboat on her back. I know I'll find other exaggerations as I read on.

Think Aloud

2 I am finding out more about the character of Sally by what other characters say about her. When the preacher says she can dance a rock to pieces, I get a sense of Sally's unbelievable strength. Sally also tells us what she is like by boasting about her own powers.

"Sally's so very special," said the schoolmarm. "She likes to whip across the Salt River, using her apron for a sail and her left leg for a rudder!"

Sally Ann Thunder Ann Whirlwind had a reputation for being funny, too. Her best friend, Lucy, told Davy, "Sally can laugh the bark off a pine tree. She likes to whistle out one side of her mouth while she eats with the other side and grins with the middle!"

According to her friends, Sally could tame about anything in the world, too. They all told Davy about the time she was churning butter and heard something scratching outside. Suddenly the door swung open, and in walked the Great King Bear of the Mud Forest. He'd come to steal one of her smoked hams. Well, before the King Bear could say boo, Sally grabbed a warm dumpling from the pot and stuffed it in his mouth.

The dumpling tasted so good, the King Bear's eyes winked with tears. But then he started to think that Sally might taste pretty good, too. So opening and closing his big old mouth, he backed her right into a corner.

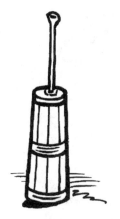

Sally was plenty scared, with her knees a-knocking and her heart a-hammering. But just as the King Bear blew his hot breath in her face, she gathered the courage to say, "Would you like to dance?"

As everybody knows, no bear can resist an invitation to a square dance, so of course the old fellow forgot all about eating Sally and said, "Love to."

Then he bowed real pretty, and the two got to kicking and whooping and swinging each other through the air, as Sally sang:

We are on our way to Baltimore,
With two behind, and two before:
Around, around, around we go,
Where oats, peas, beans, and barley grow!

And while she was singing, Sally tied a string from the bear's ankle to her butter churn, so that all the time the old feller was kicking up his legs and dancing around the room, he was also churning her butter!

And folks loved to tell the story about Sally's encounter with another stinky varmint—only this one was a *human* varmint. It seems that Mike Fink, the riverboat man, decided to scare the toenails off Sally because he was sick and tired of hearing Davy Crockett talk about how great she was.

One evening Mike crept into an old alligator skin and met Sally just as she was taking off to forage in the woods for berries. He spread open his gigantic mouth and made such a howl that he nearly scared himself to death. But Sally paid no more attention to that fool than she would have to a barking puppy dog.

However, when Mike put out his claws to embrace her, her anger rose higher than a Mississippi flood. She threw a flash of eye lightning at him, turning the dark to daylight. Then she pulled out a little toothpick and with a single swing sent the alligator head flying fifty feet! And then to finish him off good, she rolled up her sleeves and knocked Mike Fink clear across the woods and into a muddy swamp.[3]

When the fool came to, Davy Crockett was standing over him. "What in the world happened to you, Mikey?" he asked.

"Well, I—I think I must-a been hit by some kind of wild alligator!" Mike stammered, rubbing his sore head.

Davy smiled, knowing full well it was Sally Ann Thunder Ann Whirlwind just finished giving Mike Fink the only punishment he'd ever known.

That incident caused Cupid's final arrow to jab Davy's gizzard. "Sally's the whole steamboat," he said, meaning she was something great. The next day he put on his best raccoon hat and sallied forth to see her.

When he got within three miles of her cabin, he began to holler her name. His voice was so loud, it whirled through the woods like a hurricane.

Sally looked out and saw the wind a-blowing and the trees a-bending. She heard her name a-thundering through the woods, and her heart began to thump. By now she'd begun to feel that Davy Crockett was the whole steamboat, too. So she put on her best hat—an eagle's nest with a wildcat's tail for a feather—and ran outside.

Just as she stepped out the door, Davy Crockett burst from the woods and jumped onto her porch as fast as a frog. "Sally, darlin'!" he cried. "I think my heart is bustin'! Want to be my wife?"

"Oh, my stars and possum dogs, why not?" she said.

From that day on, Davy Crockett had a hard time acting tough around Sally Ann Thunder Ann Whirlwind. His fightin' and hollerin' had no more effect on her than dropping feathers on a barn floor. At least that's what *she'd* tell you. *He* might say something else.

Think Aloud

[3] *I figured out why Sally's name includes Whirlwind. When she encounters Mike Fink, the author uses descriptive words that remind me of a really bad storm. She knocks him off his feet, just like a whirlwind would in a storm.*

After Reading

Retell the Story: Ask students to draw an important event in the story, based on several of the story details. Encourage students to use hyperbole, humor, and dialogue to add to the retelling. Discuss how these literary devices add to character development and appeal.

Student Think Aloud

Use Copying Master number 5 to prompt students to identify examples of exaggeration in this tall tale.

"I noticed the author . . ."

Think and Respond

1. How does Sally show her independence when Davy Crockett first asks for her help? *Possible responses: She tells him not to call her sweetie; she says she'll free him because she wants to, not for a pretty little comb.* **Analytical**

2. What are some features that show this is a tall tale? *Possible responses: The characters are larger than life, and some appear in other tall tales; it uses exaggeration; it is set in the American wilderness of the past.* **Genre**

3. Explain why the author uses words and phrases such as *gizzard*, *varmint*, and *crotch of a tree*. What is the value of using this language in a tall tale? *Possible response: The words are colorful and conversational. They also tell about where the characters are from (the setting) and add a lot of energy to the story plot.* **Author's Purpose**

A Symphony of Trees

by Charles Ghigna

Genre: Rhyming Poem

Poetic Element: Rhyme Scheme

Comprehension Strategy: Analyze Text Structure

Think-Aloud Copying Master number 2

Before Reading

Genre: Tell students that you are going to read a rhyming poem. Mention that in this selection rhyming words are used in every other line. Sometimes poets compare the subject of the poem to something unexpected. In this particular poem, the poet compares the sounds in a tree with the sounds of music.

Expand Vocabulary: To help students appreciate the references to music and sound, introduce the following words:

> *symphony:* a major work of music written for an orchestra
>
> *choir:* a group of singers
>
> *bark:* the sound a dog makes; the outer covering of a tree

Set a Purpose for Reading: For the first reading, have students listen carefully to word sounds and rhyming patterns to discover what music has to do with trees.

During Reading

Use the Think Alouds during the first reading of the story. Notes about the genre may be used during subsequent readings.

Genre Study

Rhyming Poem: This poem includes different types of rhymes. In some verses, two words in the same line rhyme, such as *trees'* and *symphonies*. This is called internal rhyme. The poem also uses wordplay, or a clever use of words, by suggesting more than one meaning of the word *bark*.

A Symphony of Trees

by Charles Ghigna

Trees make such exciting sounds.

They whisper when we're near.

Whenever we pass by the *trees*,

This is what we hear:

We hear their branches sway and creak.

We hear the wind howl higher.

We hear a *symphony* of *trees*,

Of nature's great, green <u>choir</u>.

We hear the squirrels scampering.

We hear the blue jays sing.

We hear the robin and the dove—

All sounds the *trees* can bring.

But one thing that we never hear

When we pass through the park;

We hear the *trees'* sweet *symphonies*,

But we never hear their bark!

After Reading

Set a Purpose for Rereading: Reread the poem to have students identify the sounds of language, alliterative phrases and the rhyming words. Then have students practice the poem as a choral reading.

Student Think Aloud

Use Copying Master number 2 to prompt students to identify word play, alliteration, or rhyming words that connect to the poem's title. Ask students to explain how their examples add "music" to the poem.

"I made a connection when . . ."

Think and Respond

1. Which word pairs or groups in this poem are exact rhymes? *Possible responses: near/hear; higher/choir; scampering/sing/bring; park/bark* **Analytical**

2. How is this poem different from a nonfiction article about trees? *Possible responses: It is organized in verses, like a song; it uses rhyme; it is a work of imagination, not fact.* **Genre**

3. Why do you think the poet wrote this poem about trees? *Possible responses: to show how the sounds of trees are like music; to inspire and entertain; to lead up to the surprise ending* **Author's Purpose**

Who's There?

by Arthur C. Clarke

Genre: Science Fiction

Text Structure: Description

Comprehension Strategy: Generate Questions

Think-Aloud Copying Master number 1

Before Reading

Genre: Explain that this selection is a science fiction story about an astronaut's surprising experience while in space. Encourage students to briefly discuss any science fiction writing or movies they have enjoyed.

Expand Vocabulary: Before reading this selection, discuss the following words:

> *satellite:* an object put into orbit around a planet
>
> *stationary:* not moving, especially after being in motion
>
> *schedule:* a plan of work to be done by a certain time
>
> *cylinders:* tubes
>
> *abyss:* a space so large that it cannot be measured

Set a Purpose for Reading: Have students listen to the story to find out to whom or what the title's question refers.

During Reading

Use the Think Alouds during the first reading of the story. Notes about the genre may be used during subsequent readings.

Who's There?

by Arthur C. Clarke

When <u>Satellite</u> Control called me, I was writing up the day's progress report in the Observation Bubble. This is the glass-domed office that juts out from the axis of the space station like the hubcap of a wheel. It was not really a place to work, for the view was too overwhelming. Only a few yards away, I could see the construction teams performing their slow-motion ballet as they put the station together like a giant jigsaw puzzle.**[1]** And beyond them, twenty thousand miles below, was the blue-green glory of the full earth, floating against the raveled star clouds of the Milky Way.

"Station Supervisor here," I answered. "What's the trouble?"

"Our radar's showing a small echo two miles away, almost <u>stationary</u>, about five degrees west of Sirius. Can you give us a visual report on it?"

Anything matching our orbit so precisely could hardly be a meteor. It would have to be something we'd dropped. Perhaps it was an inadequately secured piece of equipment that had drifted away from the station. So I assumed; but when I pulled out my binoculars and searched the sky around Orion, I soon found my mistake. Though this space traveler was human-made, it had nothing to do with us.

"I've found it," I told Control. "It's someone's test satellite. Probably U.S. Air Force, early 1960's, judging by the design. I know they lost track of several when their transmitters failed."

After a brief search through the files, Control was able to confirm my guess. It took a little longer to find out that Washington wasn't in the least bit interested in our discovery of a twenty-year-old stray satellite. They would be just as happy if we lost it again.

"Well, we can't do *that*," said Control. "Even if nobody wants it, the thing's a menace to navigation. Someone had better go out and haul it aboard."

That someone, I realized, would have to be me. I dared not take anyone from the construction teams, for we were already behind <u>schedule</u>. A single day's delay on this job cost a million dollars. All the radio and TV networks on Earth were waiting impatiently for the moment when they could route their

Think Aloud

[1] *As I read this selection, I ask myself questions about it. For example, I wonder why the author suddenly talks about ballet in a story about an astronaut? Oh, I see. He means that other astronauts looked as if they were doing ballet because of the way they moved in space. By asking questions, I can check my understanding of the story and focus on the important ideas.*

Science Fiction:
Science fiction combines real science with made-up details. This type of fiction uses technology and discoveries and applies them to imaginary situations.

programs through us. This would provide the first truly global service, spanning the world from pole to pole.

"I'll go out and get it," I answered. Though I tried to sound as if I were doing everyone a great favor, I was secretly not at all upset. It had been at least two weeks since I'd been outside. I was getting a little tired of store schedules, maintenance reports, and all the glamorous ingredients of a Space Station Supervisor's life.

The only member of the staff I passed on my way to the air lock was Tommy, our cat. Pets mean a great deal to people thousands of miles from Earth, but there are not many animals that can adapt themselves to a weightless environment. Tommy mewed plaintively at me as I clambered into my space suit, but I was in too much of a hurry to play with him.

At this point, perhaps I should remind you that the suits we used on the station are completely different from the flexible affairs people wear when they want to walk around on the moon. Ours are really baby spaceships, just big enough to hold one person. They are stubby cylinders, about seven feet long, fitted with low-powered propulsion jets. They have a pair of accordion-like sleeves at the upper end for the operator's arms.

Normally, however, you keep your hands drawn inside the suit, working the manual controls in front of your chest.

As soon as I'd settled down inside my very exclusive spacecraft, I switched on power and checked the gauges on the tiny instrument panel. There's a magic word, FORB, that you'll often hear astronauts mutter as they climb into their suits. It reminds them to test fuel, oxygen, radio, batteries. All my needles were well in the safety zone, so I lowered the transparent hemisphere over my head and sealed myself in. For a short trip like this, I did not bother to check the suit's internal lockers, which were used to carry food and special equipment for extended missions.

The conveyor belt carried me into the air lock. Then the pumps brought the pressure down to zero. The outer door opened, and the last traces of air swept me out into the stars, turning very slowly head over heels.

The station was only a dozen feet away. Yet I was now an independent planet—a little world of my own. I was sealed up in a tiny, mobile cylinder, with a superb view of the entire

universe. But I had practically no freedom of movement inside the suit. The padded seat and safety belts prevented me from turning around, though I could reach all the controls and lockers with my hands or feet.

In space, the great enemy is the sun, which can blast you to blindness in seconds. Very carefully, I opened up the dark filters on the "night" side of my suit. Then I turned my head to look out at the stars. At the same time, I switched the helmet's external sunshade to automatic. Whichever way the suit gyrated, my eyes would be shielded from that intolerable glare.

Presently, I found my target. It was a bright fleck of silver whose metallic glint distinguished it clearly from the surrounding stars. I stamped on the jet-control pedal and felt the mild surge of acceleration as the low-powered rockets set me moving away from the station. After ten seconds of steady thrust, I estimated that my speed was great enough. I cut off the drive. It would take me five minutes to coast the rest of the way and not much longer to return with my salvage.

And it was at that moment, as I launched myself out into the <u>abyss</u>, that I knew that something was horribly wrong.

It is never completely silent inside a space suit. You can always hear the gentle hiss of oxygen, the faint whirr of fans and motors, the sound of your own breathing. If you listen carefully enough, you can hear the thump that is the pounding of your heart. These sounds move through the suit, unable to escape into the surrounding void. They are the unnoticed background of life in space. You are aware of them only when they change.

They had changed now. To them had been added a sound that I could not identify.[2] It was an intermittent, muffled thudding. It was sometimes accompanied by a scraping noise, as of metal upon metal.

I froze instantly, holding my breath and trying to locate the alien sound with my ears. The meters on the control board gave no clues. All the needles were rock-steady on their scales. There were none of the flickering red lights that would warn of impending disaster. That was some comfort, but not much. I had long ago learned to trust my instincts in such matters. Their alarm signals were flashing now, telling me to return to the station before it was too late . . . .

Think Aloud

[2] *I am able to understand just what the astronaut is feeling by putting myself in his place. I think about being in a suit such as this, out in space, alone, and then realizing that there is something wrong. The writer sets up the scene so that I, as the reader, expect to be frightened. This makes me want to keep reading.*

Even now, I do not like to recall those next few minutes. Panic slowly flooded into my mind like a rising tide, overwhelming the dams of reason and logic that every person must erect against the mystery of the universe. I knew then what it was like to face insanity. No other explanation fitted the facts.

For it was no longer possible to pretend that the noise disturbing me was that of some faulty mechanism. Though I was in utter isolation, far from any other human being or indeed any material object, I was not alone. The soundless void was bringing to my ears the faint but unmistakable stirring of life.

In that first, heart-freezing moment it seemed that something was trying to get into my suit. Something invisible sought shelter from the cruel and pitiless vacuum of space. I whirled madly in my harness, scanning the entire sphere of vision around me except for the blazing, forbidden cone toward the sun. There was nothing there. Of course. There could not be. Yet that purposeful scrabbling was clearer than ever.[3]

Despite the nonsense that has been written about us, it is not true that astronauts are superstitious. But can you blame me if, as I came to the end of logic's resources, I suddenly remembered how Bernie Summers had died, no farther from the station than I was at this very moment?

It was one of those "impossible" accidents. It always is. Three things had gone wrong at once. Bernie's oxygen regulator had run wild and sent the pressure soaring. The safety valve had failed to blow, and a faulty joint had given way instead. In a fraction of a second, his suit was open to space. I had never known Bernie, but suddenly his fate became of overwhelming importance to me. For a horrible idea had come into my mind. One does not talk about these things, but a damaged space suit is too valuable to be thrown away, even if it has killed its wearer. It is repaired, renumbered—and issued to someone else. . . .

What happens to the soul of a man who dies between the stars, far from his native world? Are you still here, Bernie, clinging to the last object that linked you to your lost and distant home?

As I fought the nightmares that were swirling around me— for now it seemed that the scratchings and soft fumblings were coming from all directions—there was one last hope to which I

Think Aloud

[3] By using words like who, when, where, why, and how, I can ask myself more questions about the story. For example, where is the astronaut? How does he feel? Why? Who or what could be making these strange noises? Does anything I've already read hold a clue to what it might be? Do I need to reread anything, or can I just keep reading? As I answer these questions, I get a clearer picture of what's going on.

clung. For the sake of my sanity, I had to prove that this wasn't Bernie's suit.

It took me several tries before I could press the right button and switch my transmitter to the emergency wavelength. "Station!" I gasped. "I'm in trouble! Get records to check my suit history and—"

I never finished. They say my yell wrecked the microphone. But what man alone in the absolute isolation of a space suit would not have yelled when something patted him softly on the back of the neck?

I must have lunged forward, despite the safety harness, and smashed against the upper edge of the control panel. When the rescue squad reached me a few minutes later, I was still unconscious, with an angry bruise across my forehead.

And so I was the last person in the whole satellite relay system to know what had happened. When I came to my senses an hour later, all our medical staff was gathered around my bed. But it was quite a while before the doctors bothered to look at me. They were much too busy playing with the three cute little kittens our badly misnamed Tommy had been rearing in the seclusion of my space suit's Number Five Storage Locker.

After Reading

Retell the Story: Invite students to role-play a press conference at which reporters ask questions of the astronaut, Satellite Control, and the rescue crew.

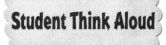

Student Think Aloud

Use Copying Master number 1 to prompt students to generate more questions about the story.

"I wonder . . ."

Think and Respond

1. Why was the astronaut so panicked? *Possible responses: He was isolated in space, yet he was not alone; he did not know what it was, yet he could tell it was some living thing.* **Analytical**

2. What details about space travel and technology make this story realistic, even though the situation is fictional? *Possible responses: It refers to real constellations in space. It refers to the use of a space station and satellites. Many of the terms, such as* propulsion jets, oxygen gauges, sunshade, *and* regulator, *provide details to make the descriptions more believable.* **Genre**

3. How does the author keep you guessing until the very end? *Possible response: He uses details that make us afraid of what the character will find, yet the ending is not what we expect.* **Author's Purpose**

Barry:
The Dog Who Saved People
by Margaret Davidson

Genre: Narrative Nonfiction

Text Structure: Sequence

Comprehension Strategy: Generate Questions

Think-Aloud Copying Master number 5

 Before Reading

Genre: Inform students that you will be reading aloud a narrative nonfiction selection. Mention that narrative nonfiction has the feel of a story, but is based entirely on events that actually took place.

Expand Vocabulary: To help students follow key events in the selection, introduce the following words:

> *monks:* men who live in a religious community

> *obey:* to follow instructions

> *patrol:* traveling through a specific area to maintain safety

> *fainted:* lost consciousness

Set a Purpose for Reading: Ask students to listen to the selection to find out how a dog might be able to save people.

 **During Reading**

Use the Think Alouds during the first reading of the story. Notes about the genre and cultural perspectives may be used during subsequent readings.

Barry:
The Dog Who Saved People

by Margaret Davidson

Today fine roads lead over the high mountains of Switzerland. Snowplows keep the roads open even in the worst weather. But it wasn't always this way.

Before the roads were built it was often very hard to cross over the mountains in winter. The only way was through some of the passes—pathways between the high peaks. One of these passes was called the Great St. Bernard Pass. At the highest point of the pass stood a big stone building. This was the monastery of Great St. Bernard. <u>Monks</u> had lived here for hundreds of years. They helped people travel safely in the mountains.

Sometimes the monks led travelers along the narrow path through the pass. And sometimes, when wild storms raged, they searched for those who might be lost. This could be very dangerous work. But the monks had help. A group of big, shaggy dogs called St. Bernards also lived at the monastery. This is the story of one of those dogs. Barry was his name.

Barry was born in the spring of 1800.[1] At first he romped and rolled with his brothers and sisters. He tagged after the bigger dogs. And he ate and slept whenever he felt like it.

But soon the short mountain summer was over. The first snow fell. It was time for Barry and the other young St. Bernards to go to school. They had some very important lessons to learn.

First Barry had to learn to <u>obey</u>. He learned to come when the monks called him, to sit and lie down when the monks told him to. He learned how to walk in the deep snow. He learned how to turn his big paws outward—and spread the pads of his paws to keep from sinking in the snow. At first he still sank in up to his belly. But after a while he could walk on the snowy crust without breaking through.

Now it was time for harder lessons. Barry learned to lead people through the pass even when the narrow path was buried under many feet of snow. And he learned one of the hardest lessons of all—to find people who might be lost in a storm.

If the person could walk, Barry led him back to the monastery. But sometimes a person would be hurt—or weakened by the cold. Then Barry raced back to the monastery to lead the monks back to the spot.

Think Aloud

[1] *I figured out that this selection is organized around time order, because I keep seeing signal words and phrases that relate to time. For example, in the very first paragraph the sentence, "It wasn't always this way," tips me off that this selection probably focuses on the past. Sure enough, in this paragraph I come to the date "1800." That's when Barry the dog was born. As I continue reading, I'll watch for more clues to time order.*

He learned to search for people who were lost under the snow. Sometimes an avalanche—a great slide of snow—would break free from one of the high peaks. It would come crashing down the mountain and bury anyone who was in its path.

The dogs were especially important at times like this. A dog could smell people even when they were buried under the snow. Then he would bark loudly, and the monks would come running.

All winter Barry and the other dogs learned their lessons. And before long the monks began to watch Barry very carefully. There was something special about the dog. He learned much faster than the others. But that was not enough. Would Barry also be brave? Could the monks trust him as a rescue dog?

At last the lessons were over, and Barry went to work. One afternoon he was trotting ahead of a long line of workmen, leading them through the pass.[2] There was a loud booming noise. It was the beginning of an avalanche!

Barry had never heard this sound before. But somehow he knew that something terrible was about to happen. He raced ahead, barking. Then he circled back around the men. He was trying to get them to move faster. And the men tried. But the last three didn't make it. Moments later the avalanche rolled down over the trail—and the three men were buried under it.

They were probably still alive. It is possible to breathe under snow, but not for long.

Barry looked at the snowy spot for a moment. Then he bounded away. A few minutes later he dashed into the courtyard of the monastery. The monks came running when they heard his frantic barks. "It's trouble I can't handle alone!" those barks meant. "Follow me!" Then he started out into the snow again.

The monks followed Barry back to where the avalanche had slid across the path. And the men who had gotten through safely told them what had happened.

"Find them, Barry," a monk ordered. Barry began to sniff across the snow. Suddenly he barked. One of the monks ran over. Carefully he poked a long pole down into the snow. Nothing. He moved a few feet and poked again. Still nothing. So he tried a third time—and gave a shout. "Here!"

Other monks began to dig. A few minutes later the man was free. He was shivering and blue with cold, but he was alive! Soon the other two men were saved, too.

That night everyone—the monks and the rescued men—made a big fuss over Barry. They praised him. They petted him. They gave him a large bowl of juicy meat scraps. And the monks nodded to one another. They had been right. This was going to be a very special dog.

One day Barry was out on patrol. He saw a small mound of snow. Something was sticking out of that mound—something that looked like the end of a red scarf. Barry raced over. He saw now that the mound was a little girl! She lay curled up in the snow. Barry poked her. Was she still alive? She was. But the cold had made her very weak and sleepy.

Once more Barry seemed to know just what to do. He didn't run back to the monastery this time. He lay down beside the little girl instead. He half covered her with his warm, furry body. And he began to lick her face with his big, rough tongue.

At first the girl didn't move. But slowly as she grew warmer she began to stir. She snuggled under Barry's belly. And she opened her eyes.

She wasn't frightened. She knew right away the big dog was a friend. She continued to snuggle close to his side—and slowly his warmth woke her up. But she was still too weak to stand.

Barry looked around. It was very cold now. But when the sun went down it would be much, much colder.

Barry tugged at the girl's coat. He stood up. He lay down beside her again. It was as if he were telling her something. And maybe he was. Because now the little girl threw one leg around Barry's body. She wrapped her arms around his furry neck. And a few minutes later the St. Bernard padded slowly into the courtyard of the monastery with the little girl riding on his back.[3]

Stories like these soon made Barry famous on both sides of the mountains. Barry just went on doing his job. He did it for more than twelve years. And during that time he helped save the lives of forty-two people.

But the work was hard and the weather was harsh. Soon after Barry's twelfth birthday the monks noticed that the dog was growing stiff and slow.

Think Aloud

[3] I notice the author not only tells me that Barry is a special dog, but she gives specific examples to prove her claim. It seems like Barry can sense what he needs to do. Instead of running for help, like before, he seems to know it is best to warm the girl with his body. Then, it is almost as if Barry is able to talk without words as he signals the girl to get up on his back.

Most old dogs were sent to homes in the warmer valleys below. But the monks couldn't bear to part with Barry. So he stayed at the monastery for several more years.

Then winter came once more. One wild and stormy night Barry was sleeping by the fire. There was a lull in the storm. The monks heard nothing. But Barry's ears were still sharp. Suddenly he was wide awake. He moved to the door and began to whine.

The monks thought he wanted to go into the courtyard. But when they opened the door Barry dashed away into the night.

Not far away Barry found what he was looking for—a man lying face downward in the snow. The man must have shouted a few minutes before. But now he lay very still with his eyes closed.

Barry bent over him. The man rolled over. He half opened his eyes. And what he saw made him scream. A big, dim shape was looming over him! "It's a wolf!" the man thought. With the last of his strength he pulled out a knife—and stuck it deep into Barry's side. Then he <u>fainted</u> again.

The old dog was badly wounded. But he still had a job to do. Somehow Barry got back to the monastery. He sank to the ground.

And the monks, lanterns held high, followed his drops of blood—back to the man.

They were in time to save the man's life. But no one was happy at the monastery that night. The monks took turns looking after Barry. At first they thought he would surely die. But finally he grew a little stronger.

Barry grew stronger, but he was never really well again. And he died a few months later.

The monks and the big St. Bernards still live in the high mountains of Switzerland. But life at the monastery is very different now. Far below, a tunnel goes through the mountain. And a safe road has been built through the pass nearby.

So the dogs are no longer needed for rescue work. But Barry has not been forgotten. Every few years an especially lively and intelligent pup is born at the monastery. That pup is always named Barry.

Genre Study

Narrative Nonfiction: Narrative nonfiction is very different from a newspaper account, even though they both tell about actual events. Narrative nonfiction gives more detail, including how people felt, and makes you feel as if you are there as it is happening, not just reading a summary of what took place.

After Reading

Take Notes: Have students make a list of details that tell what made Barry's life so remarkable. Encourage students to give reasons for including some details and leaving out others.

Student Think Aloud

Use Copying Master number 5 to prompt students to show how the author uses real-life examples of Barry's remarkable talent.

"I noticed the author . . ."

Cultural Perspective

The monastery in this selection is located near the border between Switzerland and Italy. It is one of the highest and oldest settlements in Europe. The ancient Romans built a temple on this site. In the 900s, Bernard of Menthon built a safe place for travelers on the ruins of the temple. He dedicated his life to helping weary travelers on their way to Rome.

Think and Respond

1. Why were dogs like Barry so important in the 1800s? *Possible response: There were no snowplows or roads then. In the selection there is no mention of the kind of emergency crews we have today.* **Critical**

2. What time-order words and phrases show us that Barry lived a long life? *Possible responses: twelfth birthday; growing stiff and slow; several more years* **Text Structure**

3. How do you think Margaret Davidson feels about Barry and dogs in general? *Accept reasonable responses. Possible responses: She likes dogs and enjoys writing about how they help others; she wants readers to recognize how smart Barry was.* **Author's Purpose**

CLOSE ENCOUNTERS OF THE BEAR KIND

from *Muse* magazine

by Susan Quinlan

Genre: Narrative Nonfiction

Text Structure: Description

Comprehension Strategy: Monitor Comprehension

Think-Aloud Copying Master number 6

Before Reading

Genre: Tell students that you are going to read aloud a selection that describes the work of someone who studies bears. Explain that narrative nonfiction is like reading a story, but one in which the events, the people, the setting, and other details are all true.

Expand Vocabulary: Introduce the following words to help students better understand the science of studying bears in the wild:

> *encounters:* unexpected meetings
>
> *biologist:* scientist who studies life forms
>
> *hibernate:* to be in a sleeplike state over the winter
>
> *activity sensor:* a device that detects and responds to movement
>
> *artificial:* made by human beings, not nature

Set a Purpose for Reading: Suggest that students listen to find out who has an encounter with a bear and whether it is planned or unplanned.

During Reading

Use the Monitor Comprehension comprehension Think Alouds during the first reading of the story. Notes about the genre and cultural perspective may be used during subsequent readings.

CLOSE ENCOUNTERS OF THE BEAR KIND

from *Muse* magazine

by Susan Quinlan

Beep . . . . beep . . . . . . beep . . . beep. The quickening beeps   of the radio signal tell John Hechtel two things. He's getting close to a bear den and the bear inside is waking up. Bears lower their body temperature less than other hibernators, so they're easily awakened. John and his coworkers crunch loudly as they snowshoe across the crusty snow. Bowed-down branches of willow shrubs weave a carpet of shadows over the snow, making it tough to spot the small breathing hole that usually marks a bear's den. The scientists look carefully and move slowly. It's not a good idea to step on a bear that's just woken up.[1]

John is a biologist with the Alaska Department of Fish and Game. His study area is the Tanana Valley, a boggy lowland in central Alaska. It's prime black bear habitat, but most of the ground is too wet for dens. Unfortunately, the only dry areas that seem good for dens also happen to be used by the U.S. Army for winter training. So to protect both bears and soldiers, the army hired John to find out where most bears in the area hibernate.

John spent last summer fitting bears with radio collars like the one that is now leading him to a den. The collar has a transmitter that sends out a beep John can track to its source. It also has an activity sensor that speeds up the beeps when the bear moves.

John has captured bears in traps made from 55-gallon drums. He's also darted some from the air. Darting a bear from the open door of a helicopter—held in by just a seat belt or climbing harness—sounds challenging. But John says, "No, it's not—if I have a good pilot. If I'm worried about the helicopter rotors getting too close to the treetops, then it is tough to focus. But if I trust the pilot, it's fairly simple. The more difficult part is following the bear afterward. It takes from three to eight minutes for the drug to take full effect. We have to keep close enough to watch the bear without making it panic. If the bear falls into water, then I have to get down right away and make sure its head stays up, so it doesn't drown."[2]

John and his coworkers calmly close in on this sleeping bear. The beeping signal is now strong and fast. John spots

Think Aloud

[1] *I like how the author starts the narrative. She makes it feel as if I am right there! It really grabs my attention and makes me want to read more. I wonder why they are being so loud when they are getting close to a sleeping bear.*

Think Aloud

[2] *At first I thought the most dangerous part of John's job had to be on the ground, where he might run into a bear. I would never have guessed that he'd be working from the air, too. He must be really brave.*

a small hole in the snow that he figures may mark the den entrance. Before moving in, he pulls a sleeping bag out of his pack. Holding it in one hand, he advances.

The blinding glare of spring sunlight glinting off the snow makes it tough to make out where the bear is in the hole. John crouches down, shades his eyes with his hands and puts his face close to peer inside. With a startled look, he pulls back and whips the sleeping bag over the hole. The black bear inside is not only awake, its head is right at the entrance. John hopes the sleeping bag will keep the den dark and the bear calm a bit longer. He carefully readies a drug-filled hypodermic needle mounted on a short stick. It will take good aim and a quick jab to poke the needle into the bear's shoulder muscle.

Fortunately John has had practice, so this bear is drugged safely. He and his coworkers then measure the bear and the den. They return the bear to its sleeping hole after a half hour. Occasionally, they don't return the bear. Instead, they take it to an <u>artificial</u> den at the University of Alaska, where other scientists can study its hibernation more easily.

John has tracked down quite a few bear dens—about 100, he thinks. In most cases, the bear is not so alert and not so near the den entrance. Usually, John must squeeze his broad-shouldered, six-foot-tall frame inside the den, and then, without room to maneuver, jab the tranquilizing needle into the waking bear.

Most people probably wouldn't want this job. But John feels that the chance to climb into the private world of a black bear is a great privilege. After studying North American bears for 20 years, John sees bears differently than most people do. "Bears are not vicious animals to be feared," he says. "I see a lot of the same traits in bears that I see in dogs, and even people— including curiosity and playfulness. Sure, bears sometimes attack, but in nearly all cases there are specific circumstances that explain the bear's behavior. How would you feel if you were sleeping and woke up to see a stranger standing in the room? It's understandable if a surprised bear gets a bit upset."[3]

John's main worry in his work is not his own safety but that of the bears. "I enjoy the opportunity to study and handle bears," he says. "But I also hate to hassle them. It's important to me to be sure the work we are doing is worth what we are putting the bears through . . . But I have learned that we can't just leave bears alone and expect everything to be OK. We have to know more about bears and bear behavior to protect them and their habitats."

After Reading

Take Notes: Ask students to make a Venn diagram to show what they learned from the selection. Have them label one circle *The Biologist,* the other circle *Bears,* and the overlapping section *Encounter.*

Student Think Aloud

Use Copying Master number 6 to prompt students to share how reading about bears has changed their ideas about them.

"At first I thought _____ and then I found out _____ ."

Cultural Perspective

Native Americans considered the bear a powerful spirit. Shamans, or medicine men, put on bear skin and claws as part of a ritual to ask the bear spirit to help the tribe.

Think and Respond

1. In what ways is John like the bears he studies? *Possible responses: He knows their habitat; he spends a lot of time outdoors; he is tall and broad-shouldered; he understands them better than most people do.* **Analytical**

2. The selection goes into a lot of detail about the collar. Why do you think this is? *Possible responses: Perhaps the author does not want readers to confuse it with another kind of collar; readers will understand how it helps biologists track the bears.* **Text Structure**

3. What do you think the author's viewpoint of this kind of research is? Do you detect any bias? Explain. *Possible response: The information presents the risks and dangers, the safety precautions for the bears, and the benefits of study. The author might be biased in favor of the scientific research because she says that the work ultimately benefits the bears.* **Author's Purpose**

Snakebite

from *Rattlesnake Dance*

by Jennifer Owings Dewey

Genre: Autobiography

Text Structure: Sequence

Comprehension Strategy: Summarize

Think-Aloud Copying Master number 3

Before Reading

Genre: Remind students that a biography is a true account of someone's life written by another person. Then explain that an autobiography, such as this selection, is an account of someone's life written by that person. In this autobiography, the author recalls what happened when she was bitten by a snake as a child.

Expand Vocabulary: Introduce the following words and terms to help students appreciate what the author experienced:

vision: eyesight

strained: filled with tension or anxiety

conscious: awake

venoms: poisons made by an animal

antivenin, serum: remedies for snakebite venom

Set a Purpose for Reading: Invite students to listen to find out how the author reacted when she was bitten by a snake and what this experience tells us about her.

During Reading

Use the Summarize comprehension Think Alouds during the first reading of the story. Notes about the genre and cultural perspective may be used during subsequent readings.

Snakebite

from *Rattlesnake Dance*
by Jennifer Owings Dewey

When I was nine years old, I climbed up a cliff face on a sandstone ridge in the hills north of the ranch where I lived in New Mexico.

While reaching over my head for a grip on a ledge, I felt the strike. There was stunning pain from the instant the twin fangs pierced the soft, fleshy side of my hand. It felt as if a pair of needles had been driven into my body.

I used to ride into the hills all the time, usually alone. I'd dismount and explore, trying to find new ways to the tops of the cliffs. My horse waited on the flats below, her reins looped over a piñon or juniper branch.

In the fraction of a second the snake took to strike, it buzzed its rattle. My horse did not hear the sound. If she had, she'd have bolted. She feared snakes as much as most horses do.

I slid like a rag doll down the slope. I swung onto my horse's back and turned for home, clamping my good hand around a swatch of her mane. I held on as if my life depended on it.

I urged my horse to a run, beating her sides with my heels. She was old and lazy and hated running.

Ten minutes into the twenty-minute ride my stomach backed up and I started feeling dizzy. I was afraid of falling off the horse. The earth and sky rotated. Blue mountains in the distance reeled and rolled. My vision began to cloud over. Black shadows moved across my eyes until all I could see was a tiny pinpoint of light.

I wondered if I'd make it home before I died.

My horse's reluctant lope finally brought us to the main gate of the ranch. I slid off her back and somehow got the gate open. A few more stumbling steps and I came to the big corral. Lucky for me, Bill, the ranch foreman, was there.[1]

Reaching his side I blurted out, "A rattlesnake bit me," before slumping to the ground.

"Good lord," Bill exclaimed. I couldn't see his face. His voice described his shock at the sight of me. "How in the world...?"

Bill lifted me in his arms and carried me. In a tight, strained voice he said, "I thought I told you how to keep clear of those critters. I figured you knew better than to get yourself snakebit."

He wasn't scolding. It was his fear talking. He was wondering if I would die.

We came to the Chevy pickup and Bill got the door open. He slid me onto the seat, and I screamed. My hand, arm, and shoulder pulsed with a knifelike pain that started in my fingers and shot to my brain. The dizziness got worse. I could still see nothing but a single bead of light.

Bill drove full tilt up the dirt road to the ranch house. He slammed to a stop by the kitchen door.

"Got to tell someone what happened," he said, jumping out.

"Don't go," I whispered, trying to follow.

"Got to," he said. "Be right back."

He was back in seconds, but it felt like forever.

On the way to town, seventeen miles away, I was sick. Bill stopped the truck so I could throw up. He held me by the waist at the side of the road because I couldn't stand alone.

I stayed <u>conscious</u> for a while after that, until the effort became too great. It felt as though my body were floating away, taking the pain with it.

"Looks like a prairie got her," the doctor said. "But it might have been a western diamondback. The <u>venoms</u> have a similar effect."

The doctor directed his words to Bill, not to me. I lay on a smooth, stainless-steel surface in the hospital emergency room.

My vision was changing again. The pinpoint of light was getting wider with every minute that passed.

"Can you give her <u>antivenin</u>? Can you treat her?"

"We don't have any antivenin," the doctor said, his voice as slick as the table I lay on.[2]

"I don't understand," Bill said.

"The hospital is out of antivenin right now. There are measures we can take to treat her, but we're out of <u>serum</u>."

"She's just a kid," Bill protested, sounding angry and afraid. "Just a skinny kid."

"I've seen folks pull through snakebite," the doctor said. "Even kids."

My brain spun and whirled the way a planet does.

The light in the room expanded. My vision was so wide I couldn't tell where the edges of things were. Then fear, and the anguish of pain, made me pass out again.

I remained unconscious, for the most part, for three days. I experienced some awareness. I knew Bill stayed. My parents came. I caught glimpses of faces, and I heard voices. Everything

Genre Study

Autobiography: In autobiographies, authors can tell readers exactly how they felt because they are giving a true account of their own lives.

Think Aloud

[2]*I can really picture in my mind how scared the author is here. I like how she describes the doctor's voice as sounding slick like the stainless-steel table. I can almost feel myself lying on the cold table and listening to the doctor's scary words.*

came through a mist of persistent, burning pain. In moments of consciousness, my mind was focused on the agony in my limbs. Nothing else was real.

My first full day of consciousness was the fourth day after the strike. I had no feeling in my fingertips, toes, or the skin of my scalp.

"You're doing great," the doctor said on one of his visits to my room. "You can go home soon."

"Home? You mean I'm going to live?"

"Looks that way," the doctor said, smiling. "We have some work to do, but you can go home in the meantime."

By "work" the doctor meant skin grafts, three in all, to replace ulcerated skin at the site of the bite.

When I was awake I looked at the snakebit side of my body. The swelling was astonishing. My skin was shiny and purplish-black. The tightness of it made me wonder if I might explode.

Red streaks traveled like marks on a road map over my chest and right arm. It hurt to have a sheet on me. I was feverish, and it was impossible to keep food down.

Before leaving the hospital, I asked the doctor if he thought he knew what sort of snake had struck me.

"I believe it was a prairie," he said. "And I suspect you didn't get the full volume of venom the snake had in its glands. Otherwise I don't think you'd have made it."

I pictured a prairie rattlesnake basking on the ledge in the hills where I'd climbed. It was no wonder the snake struck, with a human hand suddenly thrust into its face.[3]

Back home, I rested in a lawn chair in the yard for most of the summer. I was too tired to do much but read and sleep. Three weeks to the day after the strike, the swelling was confined to my right hand and arm, up to my elbow. The purple-black skin peeled away like scales falling off a butterfly's wing.

I slowly regained strength. The trips to town for skin grafts were scary at first, but I soon realized there was nothing to be afraid of. The doctor took tiny patches of skin from my backside and layered them over the wound on my hand. In time it was almost impossible to tell that I'd ever been bitten.

Think Aloud

[3] *I'm surprised the author isn't mad at the snake that bit her. She seems to understand that the snake was just surprised by her hand.*

After Reading

Take Notes: Have students create a time line to summarize the key events in this selection. Have them compare time lines to see if they left out important information or included something unnecessary. Discuss how the time line could help them retell the story.

Student Think Aloud

Use Copying Master number 3 to prompt students to imagine themselves in the author's place, reliving the events in this autobiography.

> "I was able to picture in my mind . . ."

Cultural Perspective

The Hopi Indians of Arizona carry live rattlesnakes during their rain dance ceremony, a ritual dance believed to bring much-needed rainfall.

Think and Respond

1. How can you tell that even as a child the author understood the danger of being bitten by a poisonous snake? *Possible responses: She immediately went to get help; she did not stop or let go of the horse, even when she felt dizzy and sick; she quickly told Bill what happened.* **Inferential**

2. The author does not tell you ahead of time that she made a full recovery or that the hospital will be out of serum. Why do you think this is? *Possible responses: It lets the reader experience things just as the author did; it creates more suspense as you wonder what will happen next.* **Text Structure**

3. What is the author's reason for telling us about such a frightening event? *Accept all reasonable responses. Possible responses: People can survive terrible events; she wanted people to understand what it is like to be bitten by a snake.* **Author's Purpose**

The Great Mall Memorials

from *On the Mall in Washington*
by Brent Ashabranner

Genre: Nonfiction

Text Structure: Sequence

Comprehension Strategy: Summarize

Think-Aloud Copying Master number 6

Before Reading

Genre: Tell students that the nonfiction selection you are about to read tells about a different kind of mall than what they may be familiar with—not a retail center, but a park with memorials in the city of Washington, D.C. Tell students they will learn the detailed history of one of the memorials there.

Expand Vocabulary: Introduce the following words to help students form a clear picture of the Washington Monument and other memorials:

> *memorials:* reminders that honor someone who died
>
> *monument:* a public place that pays tribute to a person or event
>
> *obelisk:* a four-sided shaft of stone that gradually becomes smaller toward the top
>
> *spectacle:* an impressive or memorable sight

Set a Purpose for Reading: Invite students to listen to find out why, how, and when the Washington Monument was built.

During Reading

Use the Summarize comprehension Think Alouds during the first reading of the story. Notes about the genre and cultural perspective may be used during subsequent readings.

The Great Mall Memorials

from *On the Mall in Washington*

by Brent Ashabranner

If the Mall is the spiritual heart of Washington, memorials are the spiritual heart of the Mall. They honor great people or events of the past and remind millions of visitors every year of the qualities that have made our country strong. The great Mall memorials are the Washington Monument, the Lincoln Memorial, the Vietnam Veterans Memorial, the Korean War Veterans Memorial, and the Ulysses S. Grant Memorial.

The Washington Monument, built to honor George Washington, the nation's first president, was the first major memorial on the Mall. To this day, and probably forever, the sky-piercing marble obelisk remains the most dramatic, the most exciting American memorial. Together with the Statue of Liberty, it is known throughout the world as a symbol of America. At 555 feet 5 1/8 inches (169.3 meters),[1] the Washington Monument is the tallest masonry structure in the world. It is made of blocks of Maryland and Massachusetts marble mortared together without metal reinforcement. The marble blocks are underlain with granite. The monument weighs 90,854 tons (82,405 metric tons). Its walls vary from a thickness of 15 feet (4.6 meters) at the base to 18 inches (46 centimeters) at the top.

An elevator ride to the top of the Washington Monument is a must for many Washington visitors. From there you can enjoy a breathtaking view of the city, the Mall, and Arlington National Cemetery (across the Potomac River).

If you go at night, you can see Washington all lit up—quite an exciting spectacle. And if, before you get into the elevator, you stand close to the monument and look straight up at the great white shaft, you will know what the poet Carl Sandburg meant when he wrote, "and stone shoots into stars here." The lighted monument does seem to shoot right into the night sky and almost touch the stars.[2]

Building the Washington Monument was a long, slow process. As early as 1783 the Continental Congress proposed that a memorial to George Washington be built. And although Congress authorized the memorial, no action had been taken to build it by the time of Washington's death in 1799.

Genre Study

Nonfiction: This nonfiction selection tells the history of the Washington Monument, from when it was built to details of its construction. The author gives factual information about other design ideas for the monument.

Think Aloud

[1] *By using specific details, the author gives me an accurate picture of the Washington Monument. For example, the obelisk is nearly 600 feet high. What is it made of? Where did the marble come from? I like that the answers are all right here.*

In 1833 former president James Madison and John Marshall, then chief justice of the Supreme Court, formed the Washington National Monument Society. In 1791 L'Enfant had proposed an equestrian statue of Washington, but the society did not think that was grand enough. It decided to hold a monument design competition. Architect Robert Mills, the designer of several government buildings, won the competition. His winning plan called for a 600-foot (183-meter) nearly flat-topped obelisk surrounded by a circular colonnade. Atop this circle of columns would stand a statue of George Washington riding a chariot like a Roman emperor.

Another fifteen years would pass before enough money was raised to start the monument. Then various funding and other problems halted construction. Finally, in 1880, construction began again, but not before Lieutenant Colonel Thomas L. Casey, who succeeded Mills as architect, redesigned the monument. Casey eliminated the colonnade and statue of Washington, leaving only the dramatic Egyptian-like obelisk and adding a pyramid-shaped top. The monument was completed and dedicated in 1885—thirty-seven years after its construction had begun.[3]

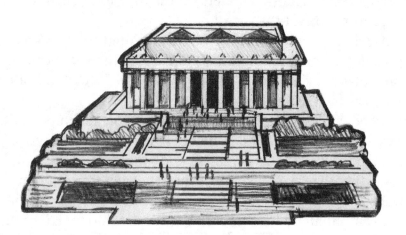

After Reading

Take Notes: Have students use the dates to create an obelisk-shaped time line of the building of the Washington Monument. Encourage students to briefly summarize the events of each year as they "build" their monuments.

Student Think Aloud

Use Copying Master number 6 to prompt students to remember details about the Washington Monument that they thought were important.

"At first I thought _____ and I found out . . ."

Cultural Perspective

In 1937, the Daughters of the American Revolution refused to let the famous opera singer Marian Anderson, who was African American, perform at Constitution Hall. To support Anderson and the cause of equality, First Lady Eleanor Roosevelt invited her to give a historic concert on the Washington Mall. Discuss the importance of Roosevelt's decision and the message that it sent to the DAR and the rest of the country.

Think and Respond

1. How might the Washington Monument have looked if it had been built by Robert Mills? *Possible response: It would have included a circle of columns with a statue of George Washington riding a chariot.* **Analytical**

2. Why are dates and other details so important in this article? *Possible response: Dates show the length of time it took to build the Washington Monument; details give an accurate picture of its design.* **Text Structure**

3. Why do you think the author wrote about the Washington Mall and its monuments? *Accept all reasonable responses. Possible responses: He wants people to know about the nation's great buildings; he wants people to picture this famous place even if they cannot go there.* **Author's Purpose**

TRADITION

from *Under the Sunday Tree*

by Eloise Greenfield

Genre: Poem

Poetic Element: Voice

Comprehension Strategy: Summarize

Think-Aloud Copying Master number 5

Before Reading

Genre: Tell students that the poem you are about to read reminds readers that poetry does not have to be formal or difficult to say something important. Eloise Greenfield uses a very human voice to show how even a simple activity such as carrying food may be connected to a rich heritage.

Expand Vocabulary: Introduce the following words to students before reading the poem:

> *tradition:* a custom passed down from generation to generation
>
> *glide:* to move in a smooth, graceful way
>
> *knowledge:* an awareness of information, facts, and ideas

Set a Purpose for Reading: Ask students to listen to the way the poem resembles people having a casual, everyday conversation, and how the poet uses this technique to explain something very important.

During Reading

Emphasize the conversational style of the poem. Use an upbeat tone, and bring out the pride evoked by the lines "knowledge came from other lands/Africans of long ago." For the first reading, read without pausing. On subsequent readings, pause to draw students' attention to the comprehension Think Aloud.

TRADITION

from *Under the Sunday Tree*
by Eloise Greenfield

Pineapples! pumpkins! chickens! we

carry them on our heads you see

we can <u>glide</u> along forever

and not drop a thing, no never

never even use our hands

never put a finger to it

you know how we learned to do it?[1]

<u>knowledge</u> came from other lands

Africans of long ago

passed it down to us and so

now we pass it on to you

for what is old is also new

pineapples, pumpkins, chickens, we

carry more than the things you see

we also carry history

Think Aloud

[1] *I notice that the poet uses very little punctuation. This keeps the reader's attention on the voice of the person in the poem. It isn't confusing, because the end of each line tells me to pause. Each line is an important piece of the poem, like a square in a quilt, or a detail in a painting.*

After Reading

Set a Purpose for Rereading: Have students reread the poem to identify objects, actions, and ideas. Then assign lines and phrases to small groups. Have students perform the poem as a choral reading.

Student Think Aloud

Use Copying Master number 5 to prompt students to discuss a detail in the poem.

"I noticed that the poet used . . ."

Cultural Perspective

Long ago the Native American Arawaks harvested pineapples, which grew wild on the islands of the Caribbean. Africans, who arrived in the Caribbean as slaves, brought new foods with them, such as okra, plantain, taro, and breadfruit. The African word for okra became the name of a stew known as *gumbo*.

Think and Respond

1. In this poem, why is the way people carry food also a way to "carry history"? *Possible response: They are keeping up a tradition that was passed down from "Africans of long ago."* **Critical**

2. Why do you think the poet sometimes uses punctuation and sometimes does not? *Accept all reasonable responses. Possible responses: Without a question mark, the line "You know how we learned to do it" would have a different meaning. The short lines show readers when to pause.* **Genre**

3. What is the poet telling us? *Accept reasonable responses. Possible responses: The things we do today are connected to the people who lived before us; examples of history are found in everyday actions.* **Author's Purpose**

Born in the Saddle

from *Born to Be a Cowgirl*

by Candace Savage

Genre: Nonfiction Article

Text Structure: Description

Comprehension Strategy: Monitor Comprehension

Think-Aloud Copying Master number 2

Before Reading

Genre: Point out to students that a nonfiction article tells about specific people, places, and times. Invite them to recall another nonfiction piece that they have read or heard, such as "The Great Mall Memorials." Explain that this selection describes a ranch woman of the Old West. In the late 1800s, the western part of the United States had far more wilderness and far fewer people than it does today.

Expand Vocabulary: Introduce the following words before reading:

> *propose:* to suggest as a plan

> *remarkable:* worth noticing, unusual

> *wilderness:* land that is mostly uninhabited

> *territories:* areas of a country that are not yet states

Set a Purpose for Reading: Ask students to listen to the selection to find out about Fannie Sperry and how she became an expert at riding horses.

During Reading

Use the Monitor comprehension Think Alouds during the first reading of the story. Notes about the genre and cultural perspective may be used during subsequent readings.

Think Aloud

[1] *The author spends a lot of time describing the horse, using many different words such as* bronc, outlaw, *and* roan. *I think I can make a connection here. I think horses will play a big part in this article.*

BORN IN THE SADDLE

from *Born to Be a Cowgirl*
by Candace Savage

Fannie Sperry admired a horse with spirit. That was why she had decided to buy the bronc that was pacing around the corral at the Herrin ranch. She liked the way his hooves stirred the blue Montana dust; most of all, she admired his strength and his wildness.

The year was 1906, and Fannie was nineteen, a slender young woman with calm, knowing eyes that looked out from under the brim of her Stetson hat. Her entire attention was focused on the outlaw in the corral. He was a mouse-colored roan by the name of Blue Dog, and none of the cowboys on Herrin Ranch could ride him. Get on board that one, they warned her, and you'll end up in the dust. But Fannie wanted to have him, and she was prepared to pay a good price. She had ridden over to the ranch on a gentle, well-trained mare, and she offered her own horse in trade for the unridable Blue Dog.

The cowboys accepted this offer and helped Fannie unsaddle her mare. There was only one small problem. Fannie still had to get back to her family's ranch up in the hills. Since she no longer had a saddle horse, how did she <u>propose</u> to get home?

Not a problem, Fannie decided. She would ride the bronc.[1]

Before anyone could stop her, Fannie picked up her saddle and climbed into the corral. Clucking and murmuring to the horse to calm him, she gently set the saddle on his back, drew the cinch under his belly, and pulled it tight. The men held their breath as Fannie swung onto the horse, but the explosion they were waiting for never happened. Blue Dog heaved and strained against the saddle, but Fannie quickly eased him into a walk. Then she turned that wild horse out of the gate and over the hills toward home.

The Call of the West

Fannie Sperry was a cowgirl—one of a <u>remarkable</u> group of ranch women who rode across the prairies of western Canada and the United States, beginning in the mid-nineteenth century. At that time, most people in North America lived in bustling industrial cities like Toronto,

Chicago, Montreal, and New York. But as the East became grimy and crowded, people began to look west. Out West, there were no smokestacks, no noise, and no fences. Instead, there was a great, shining sea of grass that supported vast herds of buffalo. These herds, in turn, supported the First Nations people, who relied on the buffalo for every necessity of life—meat for food, bone for tools, hides for clothing and shelter.

To the people in the eastern cities, the West looked like a wilderness that could be put to better use. They thought that the First Nations people should be required to settle on small parcels of land called reservations or reserves. After that, the easterners said, the buffalo should be replaced with herds of cattle. Cows would eat the grass of the prairies, and their meat could then be sold back East to the city folks as beefsteaks and roasts. This idea was the beginning of the western cattle business.

For First Nations people, these changes caused painful difficulties.[2] But for the newcomers who moved out onto the plains with their herds of bawling cows, this era marked the beginning of a great adventure. People came by the hundreds to set up ranches on the wide open plains, in territories like Alberta, Montana, Saskatchewan, Wyoming, and Texas. Among the people who answered the call of the West were Fannie Sperry's parents.

Running Wild

The Sperrys set up their ranch at the foot of Bear Tooth Mountain in Montana in the 1870s. By then, the First Nations people had been pushed aside and the buffalo were almost gone, but in other ways the prairie lands were much the same as they had been for thousands of years. The wind still swept over hills that were silvered with sage, and meadowlarks made their nests in the prairie wool.[3] Although life in the West was changing, the country had still not been plowed. (That would happen a little later, around 1900, when the ranchers themselves were pushed aside by farmers who came west to plow the land and plant crops.)

The Sperrys were cattle ranchers—they raised cattle to be sold for beef—but they also made money by catching and taming wild horses. These animals were the descendants of

Think Aloud

[2]*This information changes the mood of the selection. Life in the West was exciting for people like Fannie, but it came at a terrible cost to people of the First Nations, or Native Americans. I can see why the author tells me this. A nonfiction article has to tell the whole story, not just one side.*

Think Aloud

[3]*I think this description is important because it helps me understand what the West was like and how it began to change. The author tells about hills covered with sage, and open country that was later plowed for farming.*

Arabian horses that had been shipped to North America from Europe when the Spanish invaded, around 1500. Over the years, many of these horses had escaped from their owners to run wild, and thousands still ranged through the hills around the Sperry ranch. Ranchers like Fannie and her father would round up a few at a time by chasing a small herd of them into a corral. The first few times they were mounted, the horses tried to throw off their riders, but once trained, they became first-rate cow ponies. Hardy enough to withstand the freezing winds of December and the searing heat of July—fast, sure-footed, and strong—they were ideal for working with cattle on the grasslands.

Fannie Sperry was an expert at taming horses because she had grown up with them. When she was just a toddler, a wild horse had wandered down out of the hills to drink from a stream near her house, and she had run after it on her chubby legs, trailing a long scarf. She wanted to catch that horse! Soon her mother (an expert horsewoman herself) decided that Fannie was old enough to ride, so she hoisted her onto a gentle horse and told her not to fall off. When Fannie took a tumble, her mother dusted her off, popped her back in the saddle, and told her to do better next time. That was the beginning and end of Fannie's riding instruction.

After Reading

Take Notes: Ask students to make notes in three columns using the following topic headings: Fannie Sperry, First Nations, Old West. Encourage them to discuss which topic interested them the most and why. Ask students if they have any additional questions about these topics that they'd like to learn more about.

Student Think Aloud

Use Copying Master number 2 to prompt students to share a connection they made with a topic in the article.

"I made a connection when . . ."

Cultural Perspective

Montana, where Fannie Sperry grew up, was home to many native tribes. The Kootenai had lived there for thousands of years. They lived mostly in the mountains and came down to hunt buffalo. The Chippewa and Cree did not arrive until about the time the Sperrys did, when these tribes moved from reservations outside the state to reservations in Montana.

Think and Respond

1. Do you think the little red hen was right to not share the bread with the Why wasn't Fannie afraid to ride a horse that other people thought could not be ridden? *Possible response: She was an expert at taming horses because she grew up with them.* **Analytical**

2. How does the subhead "Running Wild" describe both Fannie and the horses? *Possible response: The horses were running wild and Fannie as a little girl also ran wild.* **Text Structure**

3. What do you think the author wants readers to understand from this selection? *Accept all reasonable responses. Possible responses: how much the country has changed; that there were real cowgirls as well as cowboys; that the lives of First Nations were forever changed as people moved out West* **Author's Purpose**

Deborah Sampson: Patriot Soldier Disguised as a Man

from *Heroines of the American Revolution*

by Diane Silcox-Jarrett

Genre: Nonfiction

Text Structure: Description

Comprehension Strategy: Make Inferences and Analyze

Think-Aloud Copying Master number 5

Before Reading

Genre: Tell students that nonfiction, such as the selection you are going to read aloud, sometimes focuses on the actions or achievements of one individual. Remind students that in nonfiction a good writer lets actual events and facts show what a person was really like.

Expand Vocabulary: Before reading, discuss the following words and terms with students:

> *enlisted:* volunteered for duty in the armed services
>
> *latrine:* a restroom, especially on a military base
>
> *honorably discharged:* officially released from the armed services when all duties have been fulfilled
>
> *pension:* money paid to people who served in the military
>
> *widower:* a man whose wife has died

Set a Purpose for Reading: Encourage students to listen to find out if Deborah Sampson's secret was ever discovered.

During Reading

Use the comprehension Think Alouds during the first reading of this selection. The genre note may be used during subsequent readings.

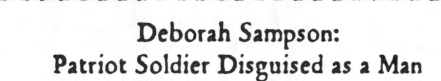

Deborah Sampson:
Patriot Soldier Disguised as a Man

from *Heroines of the American Revolution*

by Diane Silcox-Jarrett

Deborah Sampson cut her hair, tied a cloth firmly around her chest and put on men's clothes. Walking all the way to Boston, she decided to travel even further. She wanted to go where no one could possibly know her. Deborah didn't want to be recognized because that might prevent her from joining the Patriot Army. When she reached Bellingham, Massachusetts, Deborah used her brother's name and <u>enlisted</u> in the 4th Massachusetts Regiment as a man.[1]

Marching, fighting, and stalking the British soldiers by moonlight had sounded exciting to Deborah before she joined the Patriot Army. She soon found out it was hard work in harsh conditions. Her wet boots left raw sores on her feet. The food was poor. And every day she had to make sure no one discovered her secret. To do this, she could only use the <u>latrine</u> in secret or take baths at night.[2]

Still, fighting hard for her country was her goal. Deborah quickly gained the respect of her fellow soldiers. Once, during a battle with the British, she was wounded by a musket ball in her thigh. Not wanting her secret to be found out, she begged the other soldiers to let her die. They did not listen, but instead took her to a hospital. When she got there she convinced the surgeons to let her change her clothes alone. In private, keeping quiet to yet again protect her secret, she painfully extracted the musket ball from her own thigh.

Near the end of the American Revolutionary War, Deborah came down with a fever. While in the hospital she was so sick she could hardly move or make any sound to let anyone know she was alive. Dr. Barnabas Binney watched over her. He worried about the frail young boy who was his patient. While putting cold compresses on Deborah's chest, he saw where she had bound her chest to hide her identity. Startled, the doctor looked around to see if anyone else had noticed. He was the only one in the room. He buttoned Deborah's shirt back quickly and quietly treated her. Later he took her to his own home to recover.

Think Aloud

[1] *The title and the first paragraph do not tell me whether this happened during the Civil War or the American Revolutionary War. The words* Patriot Soldier *and* Patriot Army *may be a clue. I'll listen carefully to find out.*

Think Aloud

[2] *I notice the author does not tell exactly what Deborah Sampson and the other soldiers may have said. She just summarizes what happened.*

Think Aloud

[3] *I think it is sad that Deborah had to fight to receive her pension. She had fought so much already. It seems unfair that she had to fight to gain respect, too.*

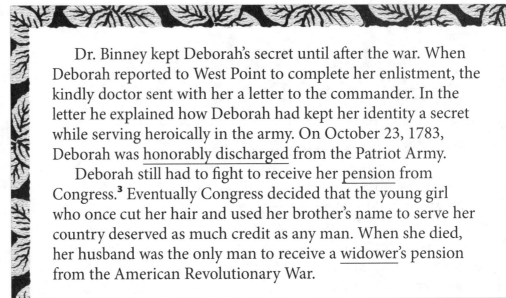

Dr. Binney kept Deborah's secret until after the war. When Deborah reported to West Point to complete her enlistment, the kindly doctor sent with her a letter to the commander. In the letter he explained how Deborah had kept her identity a secret while serving heroically in the army. On October 23, 1783, Deborah was honorably discharged from the Patriot Army.

Deborah still had to fight to receive her pension from Congress.[3] Eventually Congress decided that the young girl who once cut her hair and used her brother's name to serve her country deserved as much credit as any man. When she died, her husband was the only man to receive a widower's pension from the American Revolutionary War.

After Reading

Take Notes: Direct students to write a brief profile of Deborah Sampson, using details in this selection. Ask students to include headings such as the following: name, secret identity, where she went, what she did. Encourage them to create a heading of their own.

Student Think Aloud

Use Copying Master number 5 to prompt students to cite details from the text.

"I noticed the author..."

Think and Respond

1. How can you tell that Dr. Binney was impressed by Deborah Sampson's actions? *Possible responses: He did not give away her secret until after the war. The doctor told the West Point commander that Deborah Sampson had served heroically.* **Inferential**

2. This author uses several adjectives and adverbs in this account of a soldier's life. What descriptive words and phrases does she choose? *Possible responses: exciting, hard, harsh, raw sores, poor food, painfully, sick, frail, and heroically* **Text Structure**

3. How does this author's account change what you know about soldiers of the American Revolutionary War? *Accept reasonable responses. Possible responses: It shows that not all of the soldiers were men. It makes me wonder if there were other women soldiers, too. It shows that men like Dr. Binney respected a woman's willingness to fight for what she believed in.* **Author's Purpose**

A Visit with Kids Voting USA
by Meg Chorlian

Genre: Nonfiction

Text Structure: Cause and Effect

Comprehension Strategy: Evaluate

Think-Aloud Copying Master number 7

 Before Reading

Genre: Remind students of other nonfiction articles they have read or heard, such as "Deborah Sampson: Patriot Soldier Disguised as a Man." Tell students that the nonfiction selection they are about to hear uses a question and answer format. Tell students that the questions in this nonfiction article are what the writer asked someone named Paula Case about an organization called Kids Voting USA. Explain that the answers are in Paula Case's own words.

Expand Vocabulary: To ensure that students understand this organization's goals, explain the following words and terms:

> *voter turnout rate:* how many eligible voters who actually vote
>
> *political process:* the way in which elections are set up
>
> *polling places:* official places where people go to cast a vote
>
> *ballot:* a paper or card with a list of possible candidates and laws for voters to decide on
>
> *tabulation:* counting in a careful way

Set a Purpose for Reading: Tell students to listen to find out how Kids Voting USA promotes the importance of voting.

During Reading

Use the comprehension Think Alouds during the first reading of the selection. Notes about the genre and cultural perspective may be used during subsequent readings.

A Visit with Kids Voting USA

by Meg Chorlian

So, you just don't understand why voting is so important? Don't mention that to Paula Case or anyone else associated with Kids Voting USA (KVUSA). KVUSA is an organization that offers an authentic voting experience for anyone under the age of eighteen. With programs in more than thirty states, Kids Voting USA is demonstrating the value of the vote to students from kindergarten through twelfth grade.

Case, director of communications at KVUSA, says, "One of the very best things about KVUSA is that the classroom activities make learning about citizenship fun. And, I really enjoy meeting Kids Voting students who have acquired the skills and confidence to address something they felt was important in their community or our country." Case shared some other thoughts about Kids Voting USA.

How and when did Kids Voting USA get started?

The idea for Kids Voting USA began in 1987, when three Arizona businessmen went to Costa Rica on a fishing trip. They learned that this Central American country enjoyed a voter turnout rate of about eighty percent. A tradition of youth visiting the polls with parents on Election Day primarily was credited for the high turnout. When the three men returned to Arizona, they decided to create a program in the Phoenix area that would encourage American kids to go to the polls with their parents on Election Day.[1]

How does the organization work?

A Kids Voting program involves every aspect of a community. It is led by a board of volunteer community leaders. Organizations and businesses provide funding, election officials make an Election Day experience possible, and teachers offer activities. Students prepare for Election Day in the classroom. They learn information-gathering and decision-making skills, how the political process impacts daily life, and how they play an important role in that process. The program also encourages parent-child interaction and discussion. Students are asked to talk with the adults in their lives about early voting experiences and the general political process.

Think Aloud

[1] *That's surprising! The writer tells us that a fishing trip to another country led to an organization that encourages more Americans to vote! Unique details such as this add interest to this nonfiction selection.*

Think Aloud

[2] *I see that the author gives enough detail about the process to show me how I could try this in my own community. I'll reread it later to make sure I fully understand the process.*

Do kids really get to vote?

On Election Day, students are invited to official <u>polling places</u> to cast a Kids Voting ballot alongside the adults. Kindergarten through sixth-grade students must be accompanied by an adult. The kids' <u>ballot</u> has the same races and issues as the adult ballot, but with pictures [of the candidates] so the youngest kids also can participate. The ballot is divided into sections that enable kindergarten through second-grade students to vote on certain races, third- through fifth-grade students to vote on a majority of races, and middle and high school students to vote on the entire ballot, including issues.[2]

As the adult voting process changes, so does Kids Voting. More and more students now take part in early voting and mail-in balloting. There also have been computer and online voting pilot projects.

How are votes tallied? Are they published?

Each Kids Voting community has its own <u>tabulation</u> process. Many use standardized ballot forms, which can be scanned and computer tabulated. Some smaller programs enjoy the process of hand-counting votes and make it a community event.

All results are reported to the media just as official results are. Kids Voting programs also provide results to each school that participates.

How has Kids Voting USA seen that its program is working?

Research conducted in Kansas showed that eighteen-year-old Kids Voting participants registered to vote at a rate that was

five percent higher than that of their non-participating peers. And even more impressive, they voted at a rate fourteen percent higher than non-Kids Voting participants. Independent research also has shown that communities with Kids Voting programs see a three to five percent increase in adult voter turnout.[3]

Why do you think it is important to get kids at this age involved in voting?

We're learning that young adults don't participate because they think one person can't make a difference, that the polling place is a mystery to them, and that they don't have the knowledge and skills needed to be fully involved citizens. Recent research indicates that when students receive a compelling civics education, it leads to greater participation throughout their adult lives. By providing relevant and fun citizenship activities, Kids Voting USA is offering young people the knowledge and skills necessary for living in a participatory democracy.

Some KVUSA Success Stories

A kindergarten student in Colorado Springs walked into a polling place wearing a red, white, and blue outfit. There, she proclaimed to the election volunteer, "I'm five, and I'm voting for a woman president and am going to save the wildlife."

A mother related how she was trying to influence her young son to view a candidate the way she did. He put his hands on his hips and stated, "Mom, my job is to find out about 'these guys' and then to vote for the one I think is the best. And, voting is secret, so I can vote for the one I think is best!"

Think Aloud

[3]This paragraph is mostly about how Kids Voting USA is really working. I think this is important to know.

Genre Study

Nonfiction: Nonfiction often includes sub-headings that divide up the content of the selection. In this selection, the subheadings appear in the form of questions. These questions are then answered in the text that follows.

Take Notes: Have students jot down the notes they think would be most important to someone who wanted to organize this in their own community. Encourage students to explain why they included or left out certain details.

Student Think Aloud

Have students choose a paragraph from the selection. Use Copying Master number 7 to prompt students to think aloud about how they made sense of each new paragraph.

"This was mostly about . . ."

Cultural Perspective

In 1787 the Constitution allowed each state to decide who could vote in elections. African Americans were not allowed to vote until 1870, and it wasn't until 1920 that a woman's right to vote was made law. Have students contribute information they're learned from American History/Social Studies and create a timeline.

Think and Respond

1. How does Kids Voting USA make learning about citizenship fun? *Possible responses: They let kids vote in actual elections. They offer classroom activities that are fun. They encourage parents to help their children learn about citizenship.* **Analytical**

2. Do you think the question-and-answer format of this selection is helpful to readers? Why or why not? *Accept reasonable responses. Possible responses: No, because it was confusing at first; it would have been clearer with labels that said who was speaking. Yes, because it told you just what you needed to know; it makes it easier to find specific details when you reread.* **Text Structure**

3. Why do you think the author chose to write about this topic? *Accept reasonable responses. Possible responses: The author wants people to know about Kids Voting USA. The author probably wants to encourage readers to take part in such a program or to vote when they are able.* **Author's Purpose**

Dear World: How Children Around the World Feel about Our Environment

edited by Lannis Temple

Genre: Nonfiction/Letters
Text Structure: Cause and Effect
Comprehension Strategy: Evaluate
Think-Aloud Copying Master number 2

Before Reading

Genre: Tell students that you are about to read aloud a selection of letters. Together, these letters give readers a very personal look at people's feelings about a certain subject. The play on words of the title reflects both a feeling about the world and a feature of letter writing. Explain that while most letters remain private, published letters help us better understand what concerns other people.

Expand Vocabulary: Before reading, explain the following words and terms:

translate: to tell in one language what someone is saying in another

previously: before

concerned: care about; worried

united: in agreement or harmony

Set a Purpose for Reading: Invite students to listen to the letters to answer the two questions in the introduction.

During Reading

Use the comprehension Think Alouds during the first reading of the letters. Notes about the genre and cultural perspective may be used during subsequent readings.

Think Aloud

[1]I'm glad I listened to the introduction. It has some important information about where these letters came from and how they were collected. I know the two questions will be answered by the time I finish listening to the letters.

Think Aloud

[2]As I listen, I see that the letter writer goes into great depth. It may seem like a lot of detail, but it's all about one idea: the importance of treating nature with respect.

Think Aloud

[3]I can make an important connection here when I think about what Natasha says about pollution, even though we've never met and she lives far away. I understand her frustration. After all, we both care about the same things.

Dear World: How Children Around the World Feel about Our Environment

edited by Lannis Temple

Children all over the world are concerned about their country's resources and environment. Lannis Temple traveled around the world to ask children about their thoughts, hopes, and fears concerning the environment. Here are a few of the letters Temple collected. What do the writers enjoy in nature? What do they wish would change?[1]

To everyone,

I wish I could be an interpreter and <u>translate</u> the words of animals to my friends and teachers. I saw people throwing things into the river and also throwing all their rubbish left by the side of the river and I think if grown-ups do such things then children will imitate them and throw bits of cakes and sweets into the river and on to the side of the road. In the river we could swim in the past but as a dam was constructed, water in the river became dirty.

If the oceans and rivers could talk, I'd like to hear what they had to say about man. If I could hear them this is what I think they would have said. "We had clear water in the past but as time went by dams and factories were built and our <u>previously</u> clean water became dirty. We want human beings to be <u>concerned</u> more honestly about the seas and rivers."[2]

Sanae Kuwana, Age 11
Japan—Shikoku

Dear people of the whole world, take care of nature.

I like to swim but most of all I like watching the sunset. The sky is flooded with pink light. And the factories, as if out of spite, are puffing away and the dirty smoke drifts in the pink sky. And I want to shout for all the world to hear: "Do not pollute the air." I nearly cry.[3] And at night when it's dark and the factories are quiet I look at the stars. I am filled with freedom and happiness. And at that moment only my cat understands me. We sit and gaze at the beautiful sky.

Your friend, a friend of nature:
Natasha Manayenkova, Age 10
Russia

Hi, Dear friends,

Last night I dreamed the whole world had changed. All these dry lands had been turned into a beautiful nature full of trees, full of rivers, and the sky had become blue. War and bloodshed had ended. All the countries around the world were united, and they lived peacefully together.

I found in my dream all these trees, parks were full of trees and flowers, and kids joyfully were playing around there, and also the beautiful sun was talking to the people. Everybody was happy. Jungles were full of animals. All those animals were also happy. Nobody was sick or ill. All the trees in the streets were green. Nobody was using any car which was giving off smoke. Instead all those machines were using the energy of the sun. Suddenly, when I woke up, I found out it was a dream. But I wish the world would be like my dream.

Yours faithfully,
Hamidreza Modaberi, Age 11
Iran

After Reading

Take Notes: Ask students to list the name of each letter writer and his or her country. Encourage students to write their own letters and express their own feelings about nature .

Student Think Aloud

Use Copying Master number 2 to prompt students to think aloud about how they made sense of each new paragraph.

"I made a connection when . . ."

Cultural Perspective

Many cultures celebrate the importance of nature. Japan's cherry blossom festivals reflect a belief in the importance of appreciating the seasonal changes in nature. Have students make notes to show what each writer enjoys about nature and what they wish would change. Extend the discussion by discussing the universal feelings about nature that different cultures share.

Think and Respond

1. Whose letter did you enjoy the most? Why? *Accept reasonable responses. Students should identify the letter writer and their country, and give reasons for their answer using details in the text.* **Critical**

2. Choose one of the letters and identify the causes and effects the writer describes. *Responses will vary but should demonstrate an understanding of the difference between a cause and an effect.* **Text Structure**

3. Why do you think the editor made a point of using letters from children all over the world? *Possible responses: to show that no matter where they live, children enjoy the beauty of nature; children wish people would not allow the environment to become polluted* **Author's Purpose**

MOJAVE

by Diane Siebert

Genre: Poem

Poetic Element: Personification

Comprehension Strategy: Make Inferences and Analyze

Think-Aloud Copying Master number 3

Before Reading

Genre: Tell students that in the poem you are going to read aloud, the poet considers the Mojave Desert as if it were a real person. Explain to students that this is called *personification*.

Expand Vocabulary: Before reading, review the following words with students:

> *arroyos:* steep-sided gulches in a desert that are wet only after heavy rain
>
> *thrust:* a strong push
>
> *tread:* a footstep
>
> *raucous:* loud or grating

Set a Purpose for Reading: As students listen to the poem, have them picture the desert itself speaking.

During Reading

For the first reading, read expressively without interruption to convey the sense that the desert is a living being, almost human. Occasionally slow your pace to emphasize a word to help students comprehend more of the meaning during this first reading. On subsequent readings, pause to discuss the comprehension Think Aloud with students.

MOJAVE

by Diane Siebert

I am the desert.
I am free.
Come walk the sweeping face of me.

Through canyon eyes of sandstone red
I see the hawk, his wings outspread;
He sunward soars to block the light
And casts the shadow of his flight
Upon my vast and ancient face,
Whose deep <u>arroyos</u> boldly trace
The paths where sudden waters run—
Long streams of tears dried by the sun.

I feel the windstorm's violent <u>thrust</u>;
I feel the sting of sand and dust
As bit by bit, and year by year,
New features on my face appear.

Great mountain ranges stretch for miles
To crease my face with frowns and smiles.[1]
My lakes are dry and marked by tracks
Of zigging, zagging, long-eared jacks.
Dust devils swirl and slowly rise;
They whistle, whirling to the skies,
While tossed and blown in great stampedes
Are stumbling, bumbling tumbleweeds.

I feel the <u>tread</u> of tiny feet
As lizards dart in swift retreat
To hide in shadows, safe, unseen,
Beneath the yucca's spears of green.
Here Joshua trees, in mighty stands,
Spread twisted arms and sharp, green hands
Above the tortoises who sleep
Within the shade, then slowly creep
Across my rocks, in armored domes,
To crawl inside their burrowed homes;
And snakes with lovely, patterned skin
Go gliding, hiding deep within

Think Aloud

[1]*The poet compares the wrinkled outline of mountains to the lines made by smiles and frowns. This makes me realize that I am supposed to visualize the desert as a very old person's face. Picturing the desert as ancient is an interesting way to understand the desert's true age.*

My rocky face, far from the light,
Protected, cool, and out of sight.

Above, I hear a raucous cry
And see the bold, black raven fly
On waves of wind, to make his way
Across the endless stretch of day.
And just as far as he can see,
Creosote bushes cover me;
From limestone cliffs to white salt flats,
They shelter insects, birds, and rats.

Here, silvery mirages dance
Among the prickly cactus plants
Whose spines and bristles help them thrive
Where weaker plants could not survive.
The beavertails; the hedgehogs stout;
The jointed chollas reaching out;
The barrel cacti, fat and round—
All live upon my arid ground.

High on a ridge wild mustangs stand;
They stare across the sunbaked land,
And sensing danger, turn in fear
To gallop off and disappear.

Within my valleys, ghost towns lie;
Their crumbling walls personify
The dreams of those who used to be—
Of those who tried to conquer me.

Here, long ago, the miners came
To seek their fortunes and their fame—
To find the silver and the gold
That deep inside myself I hold.
They came to me with lofty hopes
And left behind, upon my slopes,
Their burros, whose descendants roam
On this, their harsh adopted home.

And as the desert seasons change,
The hands of Nature rearrange
My timeworn face with new designs
Of colors, shadows, shapes, and lines:

In wintertime the north winds blow;
My mountain peaks are capped with snow;

But resting, waiting patiently
Beneath the frost that covers me,
I dream of spring, when I can wear
The blossoms of the prickly pear,
Along with flowers, wild and bright,
And butterflies in joyful flight.

My summer face is cracked and dry
All blotched and flecked with alkali,
Until the coming of a storm
When thunderclouds above me form,
And bursting, send their rains to pound
Across my high, unyielding ground
Where walls of water grow, and flow
Toward my valleys far below.

But soon the blazing sun breaks through,
And then, beneath skies wide and blue,
My features shimmer, blurred by heat,
    Till autumn breezes, cool and sweet,
Caress my face, now brown and burned,
To tell me autumn has returned,
To touch the land where coyotes prowl,
Where coyotes lift their heads and howl;
At night they sing their songs to me:
                We are the desert.
                    We are free.

And on my mountains, craggy steep,
I feel the hooves of bighorn sheep;
From shelf to rocky shelf they spring,
Their hoofbeats
                echo . . .
                        echoing . . . .

I am the desert.
Feel the breeze
That dances through the Joshua trees.

I am the desert.
Hear me cry
With raven voices in the sky.

I am the desert.
I am free.
Come walk the sweeping face of me.

After Reading

Set a Purpose for Rereading: Have students listen to the poem to locate examples of personification and imagery. Encourage students to discuss a favorite line and to ask questions to clarify their understanding.

Student Think Aloud

Use Copying Master number 3 to prompt students to discuss the imagery in the poem.

> "I am able to picture in my mind . . ."

Cultural Perspective

Until the 1500s when the Spanish conquistadors arrived, the native Mojave people were the largest group of people in the Southwest. Some of the Mojave used the river to irrigate the desert soil for farming. Others made highly decorated pottery out of the desert clay and sandstone.

Think and Respond

1. What character traits would you give the desert in this poem if it were a real person? *Possible responses: patience, strength, wisdom, unyielding, sheltering* **Analytical**

2. How does this poem use personification to describe the Mojave desert? Identify an example. *Possible responses: "I am the desert" ; "New features on my face appear."* **Poetic Elements**

3. What is the poet's purpose for writing about the Mojave desert in a poem? How might that affect the way readers understand the desert? *Accept reasonable responses. Possible responses: She wants to show that a desert is like a living being that has been through many changes. She wants readers to appreciate its magnificence, not just know facts.* **Author's Purpose**

If I Only Had a Brain: ARTIFICIAL INTELLIGENCE

from *Robots Rising*
by Carol Sonenklar

Genre: Nonfiction

Text Structure: Compare/Contrast

Comprehension Strategy: Make Inferences and Analyze

Think-Aloud Copying Master number 4

Before Reading

Genre: Tell students that some nonfiction compares and contrasts two different things. In this selection, artificial intelligence is compared and contrasted with human intelligence. This helps readers understand the unfamiliar (artificial intelligence), and look at the familiar (human intelligence) in a new way. To do this, a good nonfiction writer must carefully gather and present enough facts about both topics.

Expand Vocabulary: Introduce the following words and terms before reading:

> *artificial intelligence:* the science of how to program machines to do things that normally require human intelligence

> *inanimate:* not alive

> *program:* to insert coded instructions into a machine

> *stunning:* impressive

> *endow:* to give something or someone certain abilities or qualities

Set a Purpose for Reading: Have students listen to find out which is more intelligent: a human or a robot.

During Reading

Use the comprehension Think Alouds during the first reading of this selection. Notes about the genre and cultural perspective may be used during subsequent readings.

If I Only Had a Brain:
ARTIFICIAL INTELLIGENCE

from *Robots Rising*
by Carol Sonenklar

Which do you think is smarter: a robot that can tell you what 498 divided into 328,450 is in twelve seconds, or a robot that knows how to make a bologna sandwich and pour a glass of milk?

If you guessed the robot that's smart in the kitchen, then you're pretty smart. At least that's what scientists who study <u>artificial intelligence</u> would tell you.

Artificial intelligence doesn't mean fake intelligence.[1] It means giving something <u>inanimate</u>, like a machine, intelligence. Ever since Dr. Frankenstein created his monster, scientists have longed to create a smart machine. But what does "smart" mean? For scientists who <u>program</u> robots, that question has many different and complicated answers.

In 1996 Garry Kasparov, considered the greatest chess player in history, played a six-game match against a super-computer developed by scientists at IBM called Deep Blue, or an RS/6000 SP, with specialized hardware and software designed for chess. That version of Deep Blue was capable of analyzing 100 million chess moves per second. Kasparov eventually won, but narrowly; he said afterward that the match was one of the most difficult in his life. He then challenged the computer to a rematch, which was held in 1997. Before the second match, the IBM team consulted four chess grand masters and improved Deep Blue, making the computer capable of analyzing 200 million chess moves per second.

The match began on May 3. Kasparov easily won the first game, while Deep Blue won the second. The third, fourth, and fifth games ended in a draw. By May 11, the score was tied, with each player having a score of 2.5—one point for the win and a half point for each draw. Kasparov needed to win the sixth game to win the match. But an hour into the sixth game, after the computer's nineteenth move, Kasparov resigned. He felt that he couldn't avoid losing to the computer, which meant a win for Deep Blue and gave the match to IBM.

But even after its <u>stunning</u> victory, could Deep Blue recognize Garry Kasparov if it saw him on the street? Could Deep Blue even play another game, like checkers? Nope.[2]

Think Aloud

[1] *I know that artificial means "human-made." As I listen, I use what I already know as I think about new information the writer presents. The author makes sure to explain everything clearly.*

Think Aloud

[2] *The story asks me questions about whether Deep Blue can do other activities. I don't think Deep Blue could do other things because that is not what it is programmed to do.*

[3]*I can figure out from this example that robots can't do the simple things that we do everyday. I can understand now how robots are programmed. They can't adjust their actions when something goes wrong, like we can.*

Genre Study

Nonfiction: A writer uses precise detail in nonfiction. To compare and contrast robot intelligence with human intelligence, this author carefully explains the meaning behind words she uses. Here she is careful to explain an *algorithm* with a definition and an example.

Computers can be programmed to be smart—smarter than we are, in many cases. But to <u>endow</u> robots with the kind of complex intelligence humans have is way beyond what scientists can currently do. Let's take the simple example of pouring a glass of milk. You go to the cupboard and get a glass. You put it on the counter. Then you open the refrigerator and take out the milk. You carry it to the counter. You hold the glass and pour some milk into it. Before the milk reaches the top, you stop pouring. You put the milk back into the refrigerator. You pick up your milk and drink it. That takes twelve steps. For a robot to accomplish the same task, each step would have to be programmed individually. A robot doesn't "know" that milk is kept in the refrigerator; it doesn't even know what milk is.

Plus, even if a robot was programmed to do all of those steps but something went wrong—like the glass was too far from the milk—the robot wouldn't recognize it and would just keep pouring. Robots are only as smart as the computer programs that humans have created.[3]

The process of defining the steps needed to carry out a task (like pouring a glass of milk) is called an *algorithm*. An algorithm lays the groundwork the scientist will use to program the robot. The PBS show *Scientific American Frontiers* gave an example of an algorithm that would enable a robot to pick up a cup of water and pour it into an empty cup. It would look something like this:

1. Reach for the cup with water in it.
   a. Lift arm.
   b. Move arm forward.
   c. Grab cup.

2. Lift and move the cup near the empty cup.
   a. Raise arm six inches.
   b. Move arm to left slowly.

3. Pour water into empty cup.
   a. Stop arm movement over empty cup.
   b. Turn wrist.
   c. Turn wrist back.

You can see how some things that are easy for humans to do are extremely hard for robots.

What scientists know about artificial intelligence is strange but true: The easier a task is for humans to perform, the harder it is to create a computer program to model it.

After Reading

Act It Out: Have students write out the steps for a simple activity and then follow them, showing what could go wrong. Have students write a short summary of what they learned.

Student Think Aloud

Use Copying Master number 4 to prompt students to point out something they discovered about computers, robots, or the steps in completing a task.

"I figured out _____ because..."

Think and Respond

1. Does the outcome of the chess matches between Kasparov and the computer prove that either is more intelligent? Explain your answer. *Possible responses: Yes, the computer is more intelligent about chess because it beat the best chess player ever. No, just because the computer can win at chess does not mean it is smarter at other things.* **Analytical**

2. How does the author describe artificial intelligence as being like human intelligence? How is it different? *Possible response: Machines can do many things that humans do, but not in the same way. Machines are not as adaptable.*

3. What does the author want us to learn about the similarities and differences of human intelligence and artificial intelligence? *Possible responses: Scientists can program robots to be smart, but it is hard for a robot to do things that are simple for human beings. It takes human intelligence to give a robot artificial intelligence.* **Author's Purpose**

The Mother of the Movement
(for Rosa Parks)

by Carole Boston Weatherford

Genre: Poem

Poetic Element: Imagery

Comprehension Strategy: Visualize

Think-Aloud Copying Master number 4

Before Reading

Genre: Tell students that the poem you are about to read aloud is an imaginative portrait of a real person, Rosa Parks, who is often called the "Mother of the Civil Rights Movement." Explain that some poetry contrasts beautiful figurative language and images with more realistic, even harsh, figurative language and images. The poet also chooses words carefully to create a certain tone, mood, or emotion in the poem.

Expand Vocabulary: Before reading the poem aloud, review the following words and terms with students:

> *segregation:* the act of keeping racial or other groups apart
>
> *stubborn:* difficult to move or interact with
>
> *budging:* moving
>
> *Jim Crow:* laws that imposed racial segregation on African Americans

Set a Purpose for Reading: Encourage students to listen to how the author uses word choice to set tone, mood and emotion to influence the reader.

During Reading

For the first reading, read the poem all the way through without pausing to elaborate on its references. Emphasize each new image in the poem and the mood that each evokes. On subsequent readings, pause to draw students' attention to the comprehension Think Aloud and genre note.

The Mother of the Movement
(for Rosa Parks)

by Carole Boston Weatherford

The sewing machine hums as Rosa hems
a ball gown; last task before quitting time.
Downtown twinkles with Christmas lights.
She boards the bus, takes the first rear seat
and sighs, hoping she can stay put.[1]
Segregation is a stubborn old mule,
but Rosa stands firm, too. This ride home,
she is not budging for Jim Crow,
not giving up her seat to any white man;
law or no law. Facing handcuffs, Rosa slides
her small hands out of a woolen muff,
wraps her slim fingers around a plow,
and gives that mule a slap. In the soil
of her heart, the movement takes root,
seeds of change blossom, then bear fruit.

Think Aloud

[1] *I figured out that as the poet chooses different words, the tone and the mood of the poem changes. In the beginning, the words depict Rosa as tired and weary.*

Genre Study

Poem: This poem uses both imagery and figurative language. For example, segregation is described as a stubborn mule. The author's word choice also sets the tone, mood, and emotion for the poem.

After Reading

Set a Purpose for Rereading: Discuss how the poet's word choice creates tone, mood, or emotion to influence the ideas and attitudes of the reader or listener. Have students share their opinions and feelings about the poem. Ask them to listen for words that help them visualize what they hear.

Student Think Aloud

Use Copying Master number 4 to prompt students to share discoveries they made from listening to the poem.

"I figured out _____ because . . ."

Cultural Perspective

Rosa Parks was arrested December 1, 1955, in Montgomery, Alabama, when she refused to give up her seat on the bus to a white male passenger. Her action launched the Montgomery Bus Boycott, which lasted more than a year. A decade later, the Civil Rights and Voting Rights Acts made segregation illegal.

Think and Respond

1. What images does the poet use to suggest that working for justice takes great effort? *Possible responses: The poet talks about Rosa Parks's "small hands" and "slim fingers" yet suggests how she wraps them "around a plow" and pushes the "stubborn old mule" of segregation.* **Inferential**

2. What are some of the metaphors, or direct comparisons, the poet uses to create images in this poem? *Possible responses: Segregation is a stubborn old mule; in the soil of her heart, the movement takes root; seeds of change blossom, then bear fruit.* **Genre**

3. There are many articles about Rosa Parks's historic stand for justice. How effective or appropriate was the author in choosing to write a poem? *Accept reasonable responses. Possible response: A poem can say so much with just a few words. Perhaps the poet wanted to capture the feeling, not just the facts, of the event.* **Author's Purpose**

PTOOEY!

by Linda Schneider

Genre: Nonfiction

Text Structure: Description

Comprehension Strategy: Evaluate

Think-Aloud Copying Master number 6

Before Reading

Genre: Tell students that a nonfiction selection like the one you are about to read aloud may give several examples of one idea. Remind students of other nonfiction selections they have heard or read, such as "If I Only Had a Brain: Artificial Intelligence" and "A Visit with Kids Voting USA." Point out that this selection describes how different animals use spitting as a way to survive.

Expand Vocabulary: Explain the following words and terms before reading:

> *surviving:* staying alive, especially in difficult situations
>
> *threatened:* in danger
>
> *prey:* an animal that is eaten by another animal
>
> *strands:* something long and thin, such as threads

Set a Purpose for Reading: Instruct students to listen to discover which animals use spitting to survive, and how they use it.

During Reading

Use the comprehension Think Alouds during the first reading of the selection. Notes about the genre and cultural perspective may be used during subsequent readings.

PTOOEY!

by Linda Schneider

It's not polite to spit. Everybody knows that! But for some animals, spitting is a way of surviving. So grab your goggles, put on your raincoat, and try to stay dry . . . because here come some super spitters![1]

TARGET PRACTICE

When threatened, a spitting cobra "stands" up, throws itself forward, and fires! Out from its fangs comes a fine spray of venom, aimed at the attacker's eyes. The cobra can shoot its "streaming bullets" from as far as eight feet (2.4 m). If the venom hits the eyes, it is very painful, blinding the victim for a while—sometimes forever.

SPIT NET

Spitting spiders have a great way to get a meal. They spit out a net of sticky threads to capture their prey!

First, the spitting spider gets within blasting range of a moth or other yummy insect. (That's less than an inch, or 2.5 cm.) Then it raises its head and shakes its jaws from side to side. Two zigzag strands of "glue" shoot out. These fall over the prey's body, pinning the victim to the spot. Instant prison! And it takes less than a second.

STINK BIRDS

Southern giant petrels are big seabirds that live as far south as Antarctica. They often eat already-dead animals, such as penguins and seals, along with garbage from ships. But it's what they sometimes do with their meals that most likely gave them their nicknames: "stinkers" or "stink pots."

A gull or other attacker that comes too near a petrel's nest is in for a nasty surprise. The petrel spews out a smelly liquid of rotten leftovers and oil from its stomach. It can spray this gross mixture several feet with amazing accuracy.

But adults aren't the only ones that can spit. Chicks, too, splatter a lot, sometimes even getting their parents wet. Believe it or not, the smell from petrel spit, even a baby's, can linger for up to four years![2]

WATER PISTOL

The archer fish from Asia is a real sharp-shooter. When swimming near the surface of the water, it looks for tasty insects on branches overhead. When it sees one, it presses its tongue up against a groove on the roof of its mouth. This makes a straw-like tube. Then the fish snaps its gill covers shut, forcing water out of its mouth tube—like a blast from a water pistol. Bull's-eye! Archer fish can spit-whack an insect from a distance of 10 feet (3 m).[3]

SLIME TIME

You wouldn't want to get between two llamas going after the same meal. When they're mad at each other, llamas don't often kick or bite. Instead, they spit! A llama can easily make a spray bomb. It mixes whatever is in its mouth with saliva and gobs of stomach juices. With this, the pack-animals pack a powerful *PTOOEY*! (Good thing they rarely spit at people.)

So if you see a glaring llama with its ears back and head tilted up, stand back. WAY BACK. It might be about to launch a messy green glob. *Splutch. Phew*! Be glad you weren't in the way of that food fight!

There's no denying that spitting helps lots of creatures survive—whether it's polite or not!

Think Aloud

[2]*I notice the author uses many different words to describe spitting. Here, she uses the words* spews, spray, *and* splatter. *I didn't know there were so many words just to describe spitting!*

Think Aloud

[3]*Wow! An archer fish can really spit a long distance! I think this detail is important because it shows me just how similar an archer fish is to a water pistol.*

After Reading

Take Notes: Have students paraphrase the information they have heard. Then write down three animal examples that support the main idea. Encourage students to discuss why they chose those three animals to describe.

Student Think Aloud

Use Copying Master number 6 to prompt students to think aloud about important supporting details of this article on animal behavior.

"I thought _____ was important because..."

Cultural Perspective

Most people consider it bad manners to spit in public. In Singapore, spitting is even against the law.

Think and Respond

1. How does spitting help certain animals survive? Give examples from the article. *Possible responses: The cobra keeps enemies away by spitting venom. Spitting spiders capture prey for food. Petrels spit to protect their chicks. Archer fish spit to capture insects. Llamas spit to protect their food.* **Analytical**

2. The writer uses many sound words and lively expressions to describe this subject. What effect do these have on the tone of the article? *Accept reasonable responses. Possible responses: They make the article humorous as well as informative. They describe scenes from the article in vivid detail.* **Text Structure**

3. What did you learn from this author? *Accept reasonable responses. Possible responses: I learned that animals behave in certain ways in order to survive. I learned that reading about science can be entertaining.* **Author's Purpose**

The Gettysburg Address
by Abraham Lincoln

Genre: Speech (Primary Source)

Comprehension Strategy: Evaluate

Think-Aloud Copying Master number 1

Before Reading

Genre: Explain that *address* is another word for a speech, or writing that is meant to be spoken aloud. Point out that Abraham Lincoln originally gave this speech. His language reflects both the seriousness of the occasion (mourning the death of soldiers at a battlefield) and the more formal way that people wrote during the 1800s. Point out that a good speech does not just share ideas, but also moves us to care about those ideas, too.

Expand Vocabulary: Before reading aloud the Gettysburg Address, explain the following words:

> *fourscore:* eighty; one score is twenty
>
> *conceived:* born or begun
>
> *proposition:* an idea
>
> *detract:* to take away from
>
> *resolve:* to firmly decide

Set a Purpose for Reading: Invite students to imagine that it is November 19, 1863, and they are standing on the field at Gettysburg, where they have lost friends, neighbors, and relatives in battle. Ask students to listen as if President Lincoln were speaking directly to them.

During Reading

Then use the comprehension Think Alouds during the first reading of the speech. Notes about the genre and cultural perspective may be used during subsequent readings.

Think Aloud

[1]*Lincoln is honoring the soldiers who died there during the Civil War. But I can see that this speech is really about the cause that those soldiers fought for.*

Think Aloud

[2]*I wonder what* consecrate *means. President Lincoln uses several words the same way in this sentence:* dedicate, consecrate, *and* hallow. *I know that* dedicate *means "to set something apart for a purpose." So I think* consecrate *means something similar.*

The Gettysburg Address
by Abraham Lincoln

On November 19, 1863, while the northern and southern states were still at war, fifteen thousand supporters of the Union Army gathered for a special ceremony in Gettysburg, Pennsylvania. The ceremony's purpose was to dedicate a cemetery in honor of the soldiers who had died there in battle. The people who organized the event asked President Lincoln to say a few words and it was here that he gave his famous "Gettysburg Address." Although it took the President only two minutes to deliver the speech, it is considered to be one of the most remembered and important addresses ever given.

Four score and seven years ago, our fathers brought forth upon this continent a new nation, conceived in Liberty and dedicated to the proposition that all men are created equal.

Now we are engaged in a great civil war, testing whether that nation, or any nation so conceived and so dedicated, can long endure. We are met on a great battlefield of that war. We have come to dedicate a portion of that field, as a final resting place for those who here gave their lives that that nation might live. It is altogether fitting and proper that we should do this.[1]

But, in a larger sense, we can not dedicate—we can not consecrate—we can not hallow—this ground.[2] The brave men, living and dead, who struggled here have consecrated it far above our poor power to add or detract. The world will little note nor long remember what we say here but it can never forget what they did here. It is for us the living, rather to be dedicated here to the unfinished work which they who fought here have thus far so nobly advanced. It is rather for us to be here dedicated to the great task remaining before us—that from these honored dead we take increased devotion to that cause for which they gave the last full measure of devotion—that we here highly resolve that these dead shall not have died in vain—that this nation, under God, shall have a new birth of freedom—and that government of the people, by the people, for the people, shall not perish from the earth.

In an effort to make his intentions as clear as possible, President Lincoln rewrote his Gettysburg Address five times—making changes even as he spoke at the ceremonies in 1863. The final version may be found carved on a stone plaque at the Lincoln Memorial in Washington, D.C.

 **After Reading**

Take Notes: Tell students that in every great speech certain words and phrases stand out. Ask students to note a few examples of words and phrases that reflect the Civil War period. Discuss how language and word usage has changed from earlier periods of our history to current times.

Student Think Aloud

"I wonder ..."

Use Copying Master number 1 to prompt students to share any questions they might have about the Gettysburg Address.

Cultural Perspective

On August 28, 1963, one hundred years after Lincoln's speech, Civil Rights leader Dr. Martin Luther King, Jr., delivered the famous "I Have a Dream" speech at the Lincoln Memorial. The opening line echoed Lincoln's address: "Five score years ago, a great American, in whose symbolic shadow we stand today, signed the Emancipation Proclamation."

Think and Respond

1. Which part of the speech do you think is most important? Why? *Responses will vary. Students should locate an idea in the text, restate it in their own words, and give reasons for their opinions.* **Critical**

2. Abraham Lincoln gave the Gettysburg Address in 1863. Why did he begin this famous speech by mentioning the founding fathers and the Constitution? What tone does this set for the rest of his speech? *Abraham Lincoln reminds his audience that the same country that people died for during the Revolutionary War was in danger of being divided up after the Civil War. This makes the cause a much nobler one, and Lincoln's audience is moved to continue doing everything possible to help the Union army win.* **Genre**

3. What does this speech tell you about Abraham Lincoln's feelings toward the Civil War and his country? *Possible responses: He is determined to keep the country together. He is sad that these men have died but wants people to always remember their sacrifice.* **Author's Purpose**

Nature's Fury
For Better or Worse
by Stephen James O'Meara

Genre: Nonfiction Article

Text Structure: Fact/Opinion

Comprehension Strategy: Analyze Text Structure

Think-Aloud Copying Master number 6

Before Reading

Genre: Tell students that some nonfiction selections include anecdotes, or brief stories, that support the main idea. Remind students of other similar nonfiction selections they have read, such as "Ptooey!" Explain that the following nonfiction selection offers a different point of view on the world's weather. The author includes brief anecdotes about weather throughout history to support his viewpoint.

Expand Vocabulary: Before reading the selection, explain the following words and terms:

> *funnel cloud:* a cone-shaped cloud that points down from a thundercloud
>
> *mph:* abbreviation for "miles per hour"
>
> *dissipating:* weakening, fading, or disappearing
>
> *tri-state:* affecting three states that border each other
>
> *evacuated:* removed people from a dangerous place

Set a Purpose for Reading: Ask students to listen to the events reported in the article and to take note of the author's opinion about them.

During Reading

Then use the comprehension Think Alouds during the first reading of the selection. The genre note may be used during subsequent readings.

Nature's Fury
For Better or Worse

by Stephen James O'Meara

Hurricanes, tornadoes, droughts, floods, blizzards, cold snaps, monsoons, typhoons, and more. Severe weather affects millions of people—and even takes lives—across the globe every day. And it seems to be getting worse. Or is it?[1]

It might seem as if severe weather around the globe is on the rise, in part, because of improvements in communication and technology. Thirty years ago, we did not have the Internet or cable news. A hundred years ago there were no radios, no TV. 'Round-the-clock coverage of the weather was what you observed around you.

Today we hear more about severe weather because there are more people and ways to report it . . . immediately! Weather satellites circle the globe, constantly monitoring Earth. When a tornado touches down in Kansas, a hurricane approaches Florida, or a flood washes away homes in Egypt, we hear about it and see pictures within hours.

The fact is, severe weather—even dramatic climate change—has always been a part of Earth's history.[2] Indeed, some of the storms we have experienced in recent years pale in comparison to those that occurred early in the 20th century and before. Let's look back in time to a few of the many remarkable weather events in modern history. These stories are fact and should put some of our recent weather woes into perspective.

The Great Tri-State Tornado of 1925

On March 18, 1925, the most devastating and powerful tornado in American history touched down near Ellington, MO. The hideous <u>funnel cloud</u> was about a quarter-mile in width but at times grew as wide as a mile. It was so large that some people could scarcely distinguish it as a tornado.

Shortly after touching down, the twister crossed the Mississippi River about 75 miles southeast of St. Louis. It then traveled 219 miles on the ground, plowing through southern Illinois and southwestern Indiana at 60 <u>mph</u>. It completely

Think Aloud

[1] At first I thought the writer agrees that the weather is getting worse. Then I found out that he questions whether this is really so.

Think Aloud

[2] I notice the author uses the phrase "The fact is." The writer alerts us to an upcoming point of view: the fact that severe weather is as old as time.

ripped apart four towns and severely damaged six. It destroyed 15,000 homes, some of which were lofted into the air—where they exploded like bombs. Before dissipating, the tornado had injured 2,000 people and killed 695—a record for a single tornado. Now called the Great Tri-State Tornado, the storm left behind a legacy that can still be seen today—ghost towns, solemn graves, and stories of horror that are passed on from generation to generation.

Black Sunday (April 14, 1935)

The story of Black Sunday begins in 1931, when a severe drought hits the Great Plains of the United States. As crops die and farmlands dry, dust begins to blow. The following year, 14 dust storms strike the region; that number doubles in 1933 (locals count 139 "dirty days" that year).

Then, on May 11, 1934, a major dust storm brews in the Dakotas; airborne particles sail clear across the States to the eastern seaboard. Dense sand blots out the sun over Washington, D.C., 2,000 miles away. The storm also drives grit between the teeth of New Yorkers and dusts the decks of ships 300 miles out to sea! Meanwhile, heat records soar in the Great Plains; record highs are broken on a regular basis. Hundreds of people die in the heat.

Nearly a year later, the bleak scene repeats itself. This time, the dust blows in from the drying farmlands of Kansas, Colorado, Texas, and Oklahoma. One headline screams, "The Worst Dust Storm in History." Some two million acres of farmland are evacuated overnight. Children in the Midwest scurry to school with moistened cloths clutched to their noses. So much sand falls in Kansas that an oil driller reports digging down 18 feet and finding nothing but dry powder all the way. But the worst is yet to come.

On Sunday, April 14, 1935, after weeks of devastating dust storms, huge black clouds suddenly appear on the horizon across the Plains. In no time, people are under a "black blizzard"—as dust clouds more than 1,000 feet high and many miles wide sweep through the Great Plains at a rate of 60 miles per hour. Some people think the world is coming to an end.

During these stormy years, hundreds of thousands of families left the Plains, abandoning their homes and fields.

Millions of acres of farmland had become useless. Still the dust continued to blow—but at less intense levels—until 1939!

1816: The "Year Without a Summer"

As with many major weather phenomena, a series of smaller events can lead up to a big one. In this case, the catalyst was three major volcanic eruptions that took place between 1812 and 1815. On St. Vincent Island in the Caribbean, Soufrière erupted in 1812; in the Philippines, the Mayon volcano erupted in 1814; and in what is now Indonesia, Mt. Tambora erupted in 1815.

Together, these volcanoes ejected billions of cubic yards of fine volcanic dust high into the atmosphere. Such dust partially shields the Earth from the sun's rays, but permits heat to escape from it. The result is lowered temperatures. In the annals of weather, the year 1816 is called "the year without a summer" or the year "eighteen hundred froze to death."

In brief, in 1816 people throughout the northeastern United States, Canada, and parts of Europe experienced a series of totally unexpected cold spells. These occurred continuously through late spring, summer, and early fall. Heavy snow fell in the United States in June and frost formed even in July and August! Farmers' crops were repeatedly killed by the cold. In northern Vermont, snow drifted 18 to 20 inches deep in June. Ice formed an inch thick on standing water and icicles reached a foot long! Thousands of birds froze to death.

1645: The Little Ice Age

Actually, 1816 was just one of a famous series of exceptionally cold years. Beginning in 1812, it was cold over the whole world. In fact, some scientists argue that "The Year Without a Summer" was at the tail end of a Little Ice Age.[3]

The cold streak may have begun as early as the 1200s, although many scientists believe it started around the year 1450. Whatever, says Alan Cutler, a visiting scientist at the National Museum of Natural History—the Little Ice Age was not a single cold snap but a long and complex event. "The cooling trend began at different times in different parts of the world," he says, "and often was interrupted by periods of relative warmth."

Think Aloud

[3] I notice that the author states that "some" scientists argue that this event happened at the end of a little Ice Age. Facts can be interpreted in different ways, and opinions can differ even among the experts.

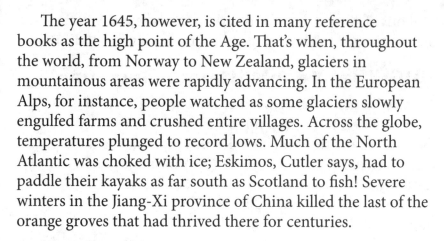

The year 1645, however, is cited in many reference books as the high point of the Age. That's when, throughout the world, from Norway to New Zealand, glaciers in mountainous areas were rapidly advancing. In the European Alps, for instance, people watched as some glaciers slowly engulfed farms and crushed entire villages. Across the globe, temperatures plunged to record lows. Much of the North Atlantic was choked with ice; Eskimos, Cutler says, had to paddle their kayaks as far south as Scotland to fish! Severe winters in the Jiang-Xi province of China killed the last of the orange groves that had thrived there for centuries.

And in the End...

So when you read news stories about "global warming" and the havoc it might cause, remember that Earth's climate has shifted repeatedly and dramatically over time spans, even ones as short as a decade—and that it is likely to do so in the future. Be mindful of how you treat our planet, but remember that . . . weather happens!

After Reading

Take Notes: Have students record their reactions to the article and the opinions that they have formed. Ask students to share these in a class discussion, citing from the text to prove their points. After the discussion, ask students whether the discussion changed any of their ideas or opinions.

Student Think Aloud

Use Copying Master number 6 to prompt students to discuss new facts or ideas they learned about one of the weather events in this selection.

"At first I thought _____ and then I found out _____."

Think and Respond

1. Do you think the writer considers global warming a serious problem? Explain. *Possible responses: No, he says that when you read about global warming, you should remember that dramatic shifts in Earth's climate are normal. Yes, he says to be careful how you treat the planet.* **Critical**

2. Why do you think the author structured the article in such a way that the weather stories followed his statement about weather having been more severe in the past? *Possible response: Because the weather stories the author cites seem to support his viewpoint.* **Text Structure**

3. Why does the author include several examples of severe weather events and not just one or two? *Possible responses: He wanted to prove that severe weather events have taken place throughout history. He wanted readers to be more informed about past weather events before they formed opinions about changes in severe weather.* **Author's Purpose**

THE HEN AND THE APPLE TREE

by Arnold Lobel

Genre: Fable

Comprehension Strategy: Evaluate

Think-Aloud Copying Master number 4

Before Reading

Genre: Tell students that a fable is a short story in which the characters are usually animals. Explain that even though fables are make-believe, their purpose is to teach a moral, or a lesson that people can apply to real life. Point out that the fable you will read aloud is also a trickster tale, or a story in which one character is tricked by another.

Expand Vocabulary: Introduce the following words before you read aloud the fable:

> *odd:* out of the ordinary
>
> *outsmarted:* used cleverness to trick somebody
>
> *pose:* to pretend to be somebody or something else

Set a Purpose for Reading: Ask students to listen to figure out what is unusual about the apple tree in this fable.

During Reading

Then use the comprehension Think Alouds during the first reading of the story. Notes about the genre and cultural perspective may be used during subsequent readings.

THE HEN AND THE APPLE TREE

by Arnold Lobel

One October day, a Hen looked out her window. She saw an apple tree growing in her backyard.

"Now that is <u>odd</u>," said the Hen. "I am certain that there was no tree standing in that spot yesterday."

"There are some of us that grow fast," said the tree.

The Hen looked at the bottom of the tree.

"I have never seen a tree," she said, "that has ten furry toes."

"There are some of us that do," said the tree. "Hen, come outside and enjoy the cool shade of my leafy branches."

The Hen looked at the top of the tree.

"I have never seen a tree," she said, "that has two long, pointed ears."

"There are some of us that have," said the tree. "Hen, come outside and eat one of my delicious apples."

"Come to think of it," said the Hen, "I have never heard a tree speak from a mouth that is full of sharp teeth."**¹**

"There are some of us that can," said the tree. "Hen, come outside and rest your back against the bark of my trunk."

"I have heard," said the Hen, "that some of you trees lose all of your leaves at this time of the year."**²**

"Oh, yes," said the tree, "there are some of us that will." The tree began to quiver and shake. All of its leaves quickly dropped off.

The Hen was not surprised to see a large Wolf in the place where an apple tree had been standing just a moment before. She locked her shutters and slammed her window closed.

The Wolf knew that he had been <u>outsmarted</u>. He stormed away in a hungry rage.

It is always difficult to <u>pose</u> as something that one is not.

Genre Study

Fable: A fable always includes a moral, stated or implied. In this story the moral is explicitly stated.

Think Aloud

¹ *I figured out that the tree is not really a tree. A tree wouldn't have ears, teeth, and furry toes. An animal is pretending to be an apple tree. It must be an animal that likes to eat hens.*

Think Aloud

² *It seems that the author wants to tell a story to entertain and to teach a lesson.*

After Reading

Retell the Story: Have students take turns telling the story from each of the characters' points of view. Discuss fables and recurring themes in literature and have students share what they know about genre and themes. Continue the discussion by comparing how different authors treat similar themes.

Student Think Aloud

Use Copying Master number 4 to prompt students to discuss what they discovered about the characters or the moral while reading the selection.

> "I figured out _____ because _____."

Cultural Perspective

Many Western fables are based on Aesop's fables from ancient Greece. India has a similar storytelling tradition. Storytellers there have told the fables of the Panchatantra for more than two thousand years. These stories were first written to educate the sons of King Amarshakti. Have students share any recurrent themes or actual fables from their own cultural backgrounds.

Think and Respond

1. What are some of the clues that the apple tree is really a wolf in disguise? *Possible responses: There was no tree standing in that spot yesterday; it has ten furry toes; it has two long pointed ears; it describes itself one way and looks another.* **Analytical**

2. What universal truth does the fable address? *Possible responses: The truth will prevail; a trickster will eventually be tricked.* **Genre**

3. This fable tells about a talking hen as well as an apple tree that is really a wolf. Yet it has a purpose. What is it? *Possible responses: to teach a moral that readers can apply to real life; to show that it's foolish to act like you are somebody you are not; to help readers understand that it is easier to be yourself and tell the truth* **Author's Purpose**

The CIRCLE and the POLES

by J. Patrick Lewis

Genre: Poem

Poetic Element: Personification and Figurative Language

Comprehension Strategy: Generate Questions

Think-Aloud Copying Master number 1

Before Reading

Genre: Tell students that the poem you are going to read aloud treats the North Pole, the South Pole, and the equator as if they were characters in a story. Remind students that writing about inanimate objects as if they are living beings is called personification. Mention that the poet also uses figurative language, or language that plays with the meanings of words.

Expand Vocabulary: Before reading aloud the poem, review the following words:

> *horizontal:* parallel to the horizon
>
> *thermostat:* a device that regulates temperature
>
> *Baked Alaska:* a dessert in which frozen ice cream is quickly baked within an egg-white coating
>
> *shoot the breeze:* chat

Set a Purpose for Reading: For the first reading, have students listen for the author's word choice and use of figurative language, rhythm, and rhyme.

During Reading

Read the poem without interruptions, using a lighthearted tone and conveying the characters through the dialogue. Then reread, pausing to discuss the comprehension Think Aloud and genre note with students.

The CIRCLE and the POLES

by J. Patrick Lewis

"I'm THE CIRCLE," said Equator,
"An imaginary line.
I circle round the planet
Like a <u>horizontal</u> spine."[1]

"You're THE CIRCLE?" said the North Pole.
"I'm stuck up here in ice,
But if we could get together, CIRCLE,
Wouldn't that be nice?"

So Equator checked the reading
On his <u>thermostat</u> control.
"Let us make some <u>Baked Alaska!</u>"
Said THE CIRCLE to North Pole.

But the South Pole interrupted them.
"While you two <u>shoot the breeze,</u>
I should mention that I'm getting
Slightly warmer by degrees."

"You are?!" THE CIRCLE said to him.
"How about a glacier melt!"
The South Pole glared. Equator flared,
Adjusting his sunbelt.

So the tropics stayed on "simmer"
As Equator let off steam,
And the Poles remained like continental
Plates of white ice cream.

Think Aloud

[1] *I wonder why the Equator calls itself "THE CIRCLE." Now I understand the poet is using figurative language to remind me that the Equator is like a circle.*

Genre Study

Poem: This poem uses stanzas and rhyme to convey playful ideas. Stanzas are sections of lines arranged into a unit that often have repeated patterns of rhyming words. In the fifth stanza, rhyming words are used to add drama to the argument between the Equator and the South Pole.

After Reading

Set a Purpose for Rereading: Have students listen to the rereading of the poem to explore the tone and mood and poet's use of humor and word play. Invite them to point out the poem's rhyme scheme.

Student Think Aloud

Use Copying Master number 1 to prompt students to discuss how figurative language provides details about the characters in the poem.

"I wonder . . ."

Think and Respond

1. What makes this an imaginative poem? *Possible response: The poet treats places on Earth's globe as if they were living beings and shows them having an argument.* **Inferential**

2. In this poem, identify and cite specific examples of figurative language. *Possible responses: A real pole can be stuck in ice. The North Pole is "stuck" because it cannot move and is surrounded by ice.* **Figurative Language**

3. Why do you think the poet wrote this poem? *Possible response: Perhaps it is meant to tell a story using facts and expressions from geography in an imaginative way.* **Author's Purpose**

Looking Back at Vegetables

by Anne Mountfield

Genre: Informational Nonfiction
Text Structure: Sequence
Comprehension Strategy: Make Inferences and Analyze
Think-Aloud Copying Master number 1

Before Reading

Genre: Tell students that informational nonfiction, such as the selection you are going to read aloud, often relates fascinating facts about ordinary things. This writer turns the subject of vegetables into an interesting report by sharing humorous or surprising facts about their history.

Expand Vocabulary: Before reading, discuss the following terms with students:

> *stew:* a dish cooked slowly in a pot on low heat
>
> *bulb:* a part of a plant from which a new plant grows
>
> *staple food:* a food that forms the basis of people's regular diet in a country or region

Set a Purpose for Reading: Tell students to listen to learn details about culture and historical time periods in the selection.

During Reading

Use the comprehension Think Alouds during the first reading of this selection. Notes about the genre and cultural perspective may be used during subsequent readings.

Looking Back at Vegetables

by Anne Mountfield

Vegetables are the parts of leafy plants that are eaten. Sometimes, they are eaten raw. Sometimes, they may be cooked by themselves, or added to soups, stews, and sauces. The part that is eaten may be a root like a carrot. It may be a stem like asparagus, or a bulb like an onion. Leaves, such as cabbage and lettuce, are also vegetables. The seeds, such as peas, or the flowers, such as cauliflower, are eaten as vegetables also. Some fruits that are not sweet are often considered to be vegetables. Avocados, peppers, and tomatoes are all fruit-vegetables.

Early people in Europe and Asia found vegetables like peas, beans, onions, garlic, leeks, and cabbage growing wild.[1] All these were eaten in Roman times. The Romans grew many other types of vegetables in their gardens. They grew beets, zucchinis, pumpkins, and turnips. Sometimes, the vegetables were boiled in water or they were cooked in olive oil.

Most people in Europe ate root vegetables, such as carrots or turnips. Farmers found that they could make the soil in fields better by growing root crops in them. During the winter, some root crops were used as animal food. Until about 400 years ago, most people could only eat the vegetables that grew near where they lived. Then, the traders brought foods back from the places that they visited. At first, they brought back root crops because these kept longer. The first carrots were brought to Europe from Afghanistan. They were purple. Carrots were thought to be so unusual that ladies wore the feathery green tops pinned to their hats.

Genre Study

Nonfiction: Writers conduct research when writing non-fiction articles about the past. This writer has researched other historical sources to find out how trade and exploration shaped people's eating habits.

Think Aloud

[1]*The writer says that early vegetables grew like weeds. From my experience, I know these plants are now domesticated through cultivation. Many changes in these plants must have taken place over the centuries.*

Potatoes

Potatoes, pumpkins, and lima beans are all vegetables that first grew in South America. The Spanish explorers first saw potatoes in Peru over 400 years ago. They took them back to Europe.

At first, potatoes were not liked in Europe.[2] The French people thought that they were poisonous. The King of France wanted country people to grow them. The King thought up a plan. He ordered his gardeners to plant some potatoes. When the potatoes grew up to be plants, the king ordered his soldiers to guard them. At night, the soldiers were sent home. People thought potatoes must be good if the king had his plants guarded. Some people crept out at night and stole the potatoes. Then, they began to plant potatoes themselves. Potatoes became the main food for many country people in Europe after that.

Vegetables in Hot Countries

In the past, vegetables that had been cooked were often safer to eat than meat or fish that was not fresh. This is still true in hot countries. Often, people eat little or no meat. Often, root plants like cassava are the staple food.[3] Sweet potatoes, or yams, are eaten widely in many African countries, in the West Indies, and the southern part of the United States.

Take Notes: Ask students to paraphrase the information about vegetables from the selection. Then cite specific details that are related to the subject, culture, and history.

Student Think Aloud

Use Copying Master number 1 to prompt students to share questions about the text.

"I wonder . . ."

Cultural Perspective

Ireland was the first country in Europe where potatoes became a staple food. However, the potato's popularity in Ireland caused a famine when the potato crops became diseased in 1845. Because the Irish relied mainly on potatoes for food, nearly one million people died from lack of nutrition or starvation from 1845 to 1848.

Think and Respond

1. How did farming and trading affect the vegetables people ate? *Possible responses: Farmers found out that root vegetables were good for the soil and began to grow more of them. Traders brought back new vegetables from places they visited. People shared the different ways they used vegetable crops.* **Inferential**

2. Describe the history of vegetables in Europe. *Possible responses: People in Europe first ate peas, onions, garlic and cabbage—vegetables that were native to Europe. Traders and explorers began introducing new vegetables from Asia and the New World like carrots and potatoes.*

3. What does the author do to make the topic of vegetables interesting? *Possible responses: The author uses humorous examples such as the king tricking people into stealing the potatoes to make the reader interested in reading about vegetables.*

All But Blind

by Walter de la Mare

Genre: Lyric/Poem
Poetic Elements: Assonance and Consonance
Comprehension Strategy: Summarize
Think-Aloud Copying Master number 5

Before Reading

Genre: Tell students that a lyric is a short, imaginative poem that creates a single, unified impression. Explain that each verse of this lyric echoes the other verses. Mention that a lyric usually has a songlike quality to it even though it is not set to music, and is often inspired by nature. It is also a very personal poem, in which a poet thinks about what it means to be human.

Expand Vocabulary: Before reading this lyric poem, introduce the following words:

> *chambered:* with many rooms or spaces
>
> *gropes:* finds one's way by feel instead of sight
>
> *twirls:* turns lightly and rapidly around in a circle
>
> *blunders:* moves along clumsily

Set a Purpose for Reading: Invite students to focus on listening to assonance and consonance in the poem.

During Reading

Read aloud slowly and clearly to demonstrate the poem's lyrical quality and assonance and consonance. Read through the poem the first time without interruptions. Then reread, pausing to draw students' attention to the comprehension Think Aloud and genre note.

All But Blind

by Walter de la Mare

All but blind[1]
In his chambered hole
Gropes for worms
the four-clawed Mole.

All but blind
In the evening sky,
The hooded Bat
Twirls softly by.

All but blind
In the burning day
The Barn-Owl blunders
On the way.

And blind as are
These three to me,
So, blind to Someone
I must be.

Think Aloud

[1]*I notice the author says that the mole is all but blind. So it can see a little, just not well. It has to feel its way as it moves through underground tunnels.*

Genre Study

Poem: In this selection, the poet uses assonance and consonance to create a lyrical quality. Consonance, or repetition of consonant sounds, can be found in the third stanza: *blind/burning/Barn-owl/blunders*. Assonance, or repetition of vowel sounds, can be found in the last stanza: *these/three/me*.

After Reading

Set a Purpose for Rereading: Discuss the effect of using assonance or consonance in the poem. Have students write their own poems using some of the same literary or poetic elements.

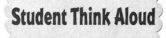
Student Think Aloud

Use Copying Master number 5 to prompt students to discuss a verse in more detail.

"I noticed the author . . ."

Cultural Perspective

In many cultures, animals have special meaning. In China, the bat symbolizes happiness because the word for "bat" and "happiness" is the same (*fu*).

Think and Respond

1. After thinking about the animals, what does the poet come to realize about himself? Who or what do you think he means by *Someone*? *Responses will vary. Possible responses: He realizes that if these animals are unable to see him, he might be unable to see some other beings, too. I think the word* someone *may mean other animals or living things.* **Inferential**

2. How does the poet use repetition in this poem? How does this link the three animals together? *Possible responses: Each stanza begins with the words* All but blind. *This links the three animals together by describing them the same way.* **Genre**

3. What insight or wisdom do you think the poet wants us to have after we read this poem? *Possible responses: Just like other animals, we understand some things but not all things. There may be more to reality than what we can see with our eyes. Perhaps he feels we should keep our eyes open and not miss all the interesting people and things that are around us.* **Author's Purpose**

Codemakers and Codebreakers Hall of Fame

from *Top Secret: A Handbook of Codes, Ciphers, and Secret Writing*
by Paul B. Janeczko

Genre: Informational Nonfiction

Text Structure: Cause/Effect

Comprehension Strategy: Generate Questions

Think-Aloud Copying Master number 1

Before Reading

Genre: Tell students that the nonfiction selection you are going to read aloud looks into the history of people who figure out codes, or systems of letters, numbers, and symbols. These codes are used to send messages that only a few people know how to read. Point out that historical nonfiction usually mentions people, dates, places, and other details.

Expand Vocabulary: Before you read aloud this selection, explain the following terms:

>*cipher:* a written code in which the letters of a text are substituted according to a system

>*operations:* organized actions carried out by several people

>*intelligence:* information about secret plans or activities

>*neutral:* not assisting any side in a war

Set a Purpose for Reading: Invite students to listen to this selection to determine cause and effect in the passage.

During Reading

Use the comprehension Think Alouds during the first reading. Notes about the genre and cultural perspective may be used during subsequent readings.

Codemakers and Codebreakers Hall of Fame

from *Top Secret: A Handbook of Codes, Ciphers, and Secret Writing*

by Paul B. Janeczko

The history of secret writing is filled with people whose work with codes and <u>ciphers</u> has been noteworthy in times of war.[1] Here are the stories of some of those figures.

Benedict Arnold was one of the most courageous soldiers in the Continental army during the American Revolution before he decided to betray the colonies by turning over the important fort of West Point, New York, to the British. Using a book code, he traded many encoded letters with John Andre, the British spymaster in the colonies. After a midnight meeting with Arnold, Andre was captured while he attempted to return to the British ranks in New York City. Because he was out of uniform, he was tried and convicted of spying. He was hanged in 1780. Arnold escaped to serve in the British army. He spent the rest of his years in London, where he died in 1801.

The Culper Spy Ring was one of the most successful spy <u>operations</u> of the American Revolution. The main players were Abraham Woodhull, who lived on Long Island, New York, and Robert Townsend, who lived in New York City. Townsend, using the code name Culper Junior, circulated among the British troops in Manhattan and gathered military <u>intelligence</u>. Using invisible ink, or "stain," as it was called at the time, he sent information to Woodhull, known as Culper Senior, who passed it along to Benjamin Tallmadge, the Continental army's spymaster.[2]

In an attempt to keep the United States from entering World War I, the German foreign minister, Arthur Zimmermann, sent a telegram to the German ambassador in Mexico outlining his plan. The Zimmermann Telegram asked that Mexico declare war on the United States. Then, because the United States would need to send troops to defend its southern border from Mexico, it

Think Aloud

[1] I wonder why codes and ciphers were important in times of war. If I keep reading I should be able to discover what role codes and ciphers played in history.

Think Aloud

[2] I wonder what the ink was made from and what the codebreakers did to the paper so they could make the ink visible. This makes me want to find out more after I read the article.

would be unable to commit troops to the war in Europe. British codebreakers cracked the encoded telegram and presented its information to President Wilson. On April 2, 1917, the United States declared war on Germany.

The Lucy Spy Ring operated out of Switzerland in World War II on behalf of Russia, Germany's enemy on the Eastern Front. The spy ring got its name from its leader, whose code name was Lucy. The Lucy Spy Ring was successful for a number of reasons. For example, the members of the ring used a number of go-betweens, so the members did not know all the other members in the ring. And when they did meet, the meetings were brief and held in public places, like cafes. For another thing, they knew the other members in the ring only by their code names.[3] When the Nazis realized that the spy ring was operating out of neutral Switzerland, they demanded that the Swiss arrest them. Some members of the spy ring were arrested, but Nazi Germany collapsed before any of them could be convicted of spying.

The Enigma was a cipher machine that played an important part in World War II. Created by Germany, the Enigma machine was about the size of a standard typewriter of the day. An agent typed in the message. Electrical impulses generated each time a letter was struck turned one or more of three rotors inside the machine, which enciphered the message in a random manner. It was the codebreakers at Bletchley Park, not far from London, who, after long and hard work, managed to unlock the secret of the Enigma.

The Japanese military had bought an Enigma machine and modified it to create its own code machine, which the American codebreakers called Purple. Because the Japanese version of the Enigma had been changed, it was much more difficult to break. Two Americans, Herbert O. Yardley and William Friedman, put together a codebreaking team as skilled as its British counterpart. In fact, Friedman referred to his gang of codebreakers as "magicians." From that nickname came the code name for all the intelligence that came from Purple: Magic.

Think Aloud

[3] *I wonder if the true identity of Lucy was ever made public. Since Lucy was just a code name, it could have been a man or a woman.*

Genre Study

Nonfiction: An informational nonfiction article is factual and detailed. Nonfiction writers do not explain every single detail, because a good reader can find out more by using other reference sources.

Take Notes: Have students use an idea map to track the different spy operations as you reread the selection. Use questioning to see how detailed students' idea maps are.

Student Think Aloud

Use Copying Master number 1 to prompt students to share their questions about the article.

"I wonder ..."

Cultural Perspective

During World War II, the U.S. military used the Navajo language as a cipher. More than four hundred Navajo served in the Marines, transmitting messages in their language. Not one of Japan's best codebreakers was able to decipher it. Ask students if they know any additional information about Navajo codetalkers.

Think and Respond

1. This nonfiction selection mentions many different spies and codebreakers. How were all of these spies alike? *Possible responses: They took risks. They had to keep secrets. They tried not to let people find out who they really were or what they were doing.* **Critical**

2. How did the story show how codes and ciphers affected history? *Possible responses: It explains who the spies were working against, when the operation took place, and whether it succeeded or failed.* **Text Structure**

3. Why do you think the author wrote this article? *Possible responses: Perhaps he wanted to show that spying has gone on for a long time and that spying happens in real life, not just in fiction. He also shows how people sent coded messages before the invention of the Internet and the telephone.* **Author's Purpose**

HOW THE WHALE GOT HIS THROAT

by Rudyard Kipling

Genre: Pourquoi Tale

Comprehension Strategy: Generate Questions

Think-Aloud Copying Master number 6

Before Reading

Genre: Tell students that pourquoi tales are stories that explain why something is the way it is. Share with students that the word *pourquoi* is French for "why." Rudyard Kipling liked pourquoi tales and enjoyed coming up with farfetched explanations for natural phenomena.

Expand Vocabulary: Before reading this pourquoi tale, discuss the following words:

> *suspenders:* straps that hold up a pair of pants
>
> *infinite:* limitless
>
> *resource:* skill at finding solutions to problems
>
> *sagacity:* wisdom

Set a Purpose for Reading: Ask students to read to find out how the whale got his throat.

During Reading

Use the comprehension Think Alouds during the first reading of the story. Notes about the genre and cultural perspective may be used during subsequent readings.

HOW THE WHALE GOT HIS THROAT

by Rudyard Kipling

In the sea, once upon a time, O my Best Beloved, there was a Whale, and he ate fishes. He ate the starfish and the garfish, and the crab and the dab, and the plaice and the dace, and the skate and his mate, and the mackereel and the pickereel, and the really truly twirly-whirly eel.[1] All the fishes he could find in all the sea he ate with his mouth—so! Till at last there was only one small fish left in all the sea, and he was a small 'Stute Fish, and he swam a little behind the Whale's right ear, so as to be out of harm's way. Then the Whale stood up on his tail and said, 'I'm hungry.' And the small 'Stute Fish said in a small 'stute voice, 'Noble and generous Cetacean, have you ever tasted Man?'

'No,' said the Whale. 'What is it like?'

'Nice,' said the small 'Stute Fish. 'Nice but nubbly.'

'Then fetch me some,' said the Whale, and he made the sea froth up with his tail.

'One at a time is enough,' said the 'Stute Fish. 'If you swim to latitude Fifty North, longitude Forty West (that is Magic), you will find, sitting *on* a raft, *in* the middle of the sea, with nothing on but a pair of blue canvas breeches, a pair of suspenders (you must *not* forget the suspenders, Best Beloved), and a jack-knife, one shipwrecked Mariner, who, it is only fair to tell you, is a man of infinite-resource-and-sagacity.'[2]

So the Whale swam and swam to latitude Fifty North, longitude Forty West, as fast as he could swim, and *on* a raft, *in* the middle of the sea, *with* nothing to wear except a pair of blue canvas breeches, a pair of suspenders (you must particularly remember the suspenders, Best Beloved), *and* a jack-knife, he found one single, solitary shipwrecked Mariner, trailing his toes in the water. (He had his Mummy's leave to paddle, or else he would never have done it, because he was a man of infinite-resource-and-sagacity.)

Then the Whale opened his mouth back and back and back till it nearly touched his tail, and he swallowed the shipwrecked Mariner, and the raft he was sitting on, and his blue canvas breeches, and the suspenders (which you *must* not forget), *and* the jack-knife—He swallowed them all down into his warm, dark, inside cupboards, and then he smacked his lips—so, and turned round three times on his tail.

But as soon as the Mariner, who was a man of infinite-resource-and-sagacity, found himself truly inside the Whale's warm, dark, inside cupboards, he stumped and he jumped and he thumped and he bumped, and he pranced and he danced, and he banged and he clanged, and he hit and he bit, and he leaped and he creeped, and he prowled and he howled, and he hopped and he dropped, and he cried and he sighed, and he crawled and he bawled, and he stepped and he lepped, and he danced hornpipes where he shouldn't, and the Whale felt most unhappy indeed.[3] (*Have* you forgotten the suspenders?)

So he said to the 'Stute Fish, 'This man is very nubbly, and besides he is making me hiccough. What shall I do?'

'Tell him to come out,' said the 'Stute Fish.

So the Whale called down his own throat to the shipwrecked Mariner, 'Come out and behave yourself. I've got the hiccoughs.'

'Nay, nay!' said the Mariner. 'Not so, but far otherwise. Take me to my natal-shore and the white-cliffs-of-Albion, and I'll think about it.' And he began to dance more than ever.

'You had better take him home,' said the 'Stute Fish to the Whale. 'I ought to have warned you that he is a man of infinite-resource-and-sagacity.'

So the Whale swam and swam and swam, with both flippers and his tail, as hard as he could for the hiccoughs; and at last he saw the Mariner's natal-shore and the white-cliffs-of-Albion, and he rushed half-way up the beach, and opened his mouth wide and wide and wide, and said, 'Change here for Winchester, Ashuelot, Nashua, Keene, and stations on the *Fitch*burg Road'; and just as he said 'Fitch' the Mariner walked out of his mouth. But while the Whale had been swimming, the Mariner, who was indeed a person of infinite-resource-and-sagacity, had taken his jack-knife and cut up the raft into a little square grating all running criss-cross, and he had tied it firm with his suspenders (*now* you know why you were not to forget the suspenders!), and he dragged that grating good and tight into the Whale's throat,

Think Aloud

[3] *I can tell that this is a lighthearted story because of the way the author uses rhyme and repetition. He also uses nonsense words to show humor, such as lepped.*

and there it stuck! Then he recited the following *Sloka,* which, as you have not heard it, I will now proceed to relate—

> By means of a grating
> I have stopped your ating.

For the Mariner he was also an Hi-ber-ni-an. And he stepped out on the shingle, and went home to his Mother, who had given him leave to trail his toes in the water; and he married and lived happily ever afterward. So did the Whale. But from that day on, the grating in his throat, which he could neither cough up nor swallow down, prevented him eating anything except very, very small fish; and that is the reason why whales nowadays never eat men or boys or little girls.

The small 'Stute Fish went and hid himself in the mud under the Door-sills of the Equator. He was afraid that the Whale might be angry with him.

The Sailor took the jack-knife home. He was wearing the blue canvas breeches when he walked out on the shingle. The suspenders were left behind, you see, to tie the grating with; and that is the end of *that* tale.

After Reading

Retell the Story: Have students retell the story with a partner as if they were the descendants of the Mariner. Encourage them to pass the legend back and forth, each telling a small part and then letting the other take over, prompting each other to recall what happens next.

Student Think Aloud

Use Copying Master number 6 to prompt students to discuss important events or details in the story.

"At first I thought _____ and then I found out . . ."

Cultural Perspective

Rudyard Kipling was a British writer during the age of the British Empire in the late 19th century. Even though he wrote in English, his words are regional and might sound unusual to readers today. The author shares that the Mariner was Hi-ber-ni-an. Hibernia is an old name for Ireland, so the word *Hibernian* means that the man is Irish.

Think and Respond

1. Why did the 'Stute Fish tell the whale about a man who was far away on a raft? *Possible response: Perhaps he wanted to save his own life.* **Inferential**

2. How is this pourquoi tale like the tall tale "Sally Ann Thunder Ann"? How is it different? *Possible responses: They both use exaggeration and storytelling features. The pourquoi tale tells why whales only eat small things, while the tall tale describes unusual characters. The pourquoi tale also has talking animals.* **Genre**

3. Who do you think the author is referring to when he says *O my Best Beloved* and *Best Beloved*? Why does he do this? *Responses will vary. Possible responses: I think he is referring to a child, maybe his own. I think he is telling this story to entertain this person he loves.* **Author's Purpose**

Yeh-hsien

a Chinese fairy tale
retold by Judy Sierra

Genre: Fairy Tale

Comprehension Strategy: Plot, Setting, Character

Think-Aloud Copying Master number 6

Before Reading

Genre: Tell students that fairy tales are stories that have been told and retold to children for many generations. They often have a main character who experiences sudden good fortune. Explain that different versions of similar fairy tales exist in many cultures. Point out that each culture adds its own history, environment, traditions, crafts, and foods to fairy tales.

Expand Vocabulary: Introduce the following words before you read aloud the fairy tale:

> *dynasties:* series of rulers from different generations of the same family
>
> *dung-hill:* a pile of waste, especially from animals
>
> *descended:* came down
>
> *consoled:* comforted someone who was upset
>
> *suspected:* thought that something was likely

Set a Purpose for Reading: Have students listen to learn the plot and decide which fairy tale Yeh-hsien (pronounced Yay shen) reminds them of (Cinderella).

During Reading

Use the comprehension Think Alouds during the first reading of the fairy tale. Notes about the genre and cultural perspective may be used during subsequent readings.

Yeh-hsien

a Chinese fairy tale
retold by Judy Sierra

Among the people of the south there is a tradition that before the Ch'in and Han dynasties there lived a cave-master called Wu. People called the place the Wu cave. He had two wives. One wife died. She had a daughter called Yeh-hsien, who from childhood was intelligent and good at making pottery on the wheel. Her father loved her. After some years the father died, and she was ill-treated by her stepmother, who would always order her to collect firewood in dangerous places and draw water from deep pools.[1] Once Yeh-hsien caught a fish about two inches long, with red fins and golden eyes. She put it into a bowl of water. It grew bigger every day, and after she had changed the bowl several times, she could find no bowl big enough for it, so she threw it back into the pond. Whatever food was left over from meals she put into the water to feed it. When Yeh-hsien came to the pond, the fish always swam up and rested its head on the bank, but when anyone else came, it would not come out.

The stepmother watched for the fish, but it did not once appear. So she tricked the girl, saying, "Haven't you worked hard! I am going to give you a new dress." She then made the girl change out of her tattered clothing. Afterwards she sent her to get water from a spring that was very far away. The stepmother put on Yeh-hsien's clothes, hid a sharp knife up her sleeve, and went to the pond. She called to the fish. The fish at once put its head out, and she chopped it off and killed it. The fish was now more than ten feet long. She cooked it, and when she served it up, it tasted twice as good as an ordinary fish. She hid the bones under the dung-hill.

The next day, when the girl came to the pond, no fish appeared. The girl ran out into the fields, howling with grief. Suddenly there appeared a man with his hair loose over his shoulders, dressed in coarse clothes.[2] He descended from the sky, and he consoled her, saying, "Don't cry so! Your stepmother has killed the fish and its bones are under the dung-heap. Go back, take the fish's bones and hide them in your room. Whatever you want, you have only to ask

Think Aloud

[1] *The way the stepmother treats Yeh-hsien reminds me of another story. I wonder if there will be a ball where Yeh-hsien loses a glass slipper.*

Think Aloud

[2] *I wonder who the man is. Could he be a wizard, a god, or the spirit of the fish itself? He is very wise and knows what Yeh-hsien should do.*

Think Aloud

[3] *At first I thought Yeh-hsien would be the only one who could use the fish bones. But here I find out that the king could also ask the bones for jade and pearls. This surprises me because this detail is not like the version of this fairy tale I know.*

the fish bones for it." The girl followed his advice, and from then on she was able to provide herself with gold, pearls, dresses, and food whenever she wanted them.

When the time came for the cave festival, the stepmother took her own daughter with her, and left Yeh-hsien to keep watch over the fruit trees in the garden. The girl waited until they were far away, and then she followed them, wearing a cloak of material spun from kingfisher feathers and shoes of gold. Her stepsister saw her and said to the stepmother, "That girl looks like my sister." The stepmother suspected the same thing. The girl was aware of this and went away in such a hurry that she lost one shoe. It was picked up by one of the people of the cave. When the stepmother got home, she found the girl asleep, with her arms round one of the trees in the garden, and thought no more about it.

The cave was near an island in the sea, and on this island was a kingdom called T'o-han. The man who had picked up the gold shoe sold it in T'o-han, and it was brought to the king. He ordered all the women of the court to put it on, but it was too small even for the one among them that had the smallest foot. He then ordered all the women in his kingdom to try it on, but there was not one that it fitted. It was as light as down, and it made no noise even when treading on stone. His search finally took him to the place where Yeh-hsien lived with her stepmother, and the shoe fitted her perfectly. She put on the other shoe, and her cape of feathers, and she was as beautiful as a heavenly being. Taking the fish bones with her, she returned with the king to T'o-han and became his chief wife. The first year, the king was very greedy and asked the fish bones for jade and pearls without limit.[3] The next year, the fish bones no longer granted his requests. He buried them by the sea shore and covered them with a hundred bushels of pearls, and after a while they were washed away by the tide.

The stepmother and stepsister were struck by flying rocks, and died. The cave people buried them in a stone pit, which was called the Tomb of the Two Women. Men would come there and make offerings, and the girl they prayed for would become their wife.

Retell the Story: Ask students what the point of view of the story is. Then have students take turns telling the story from one of the following points of view: the narrator, Yeh-hsien, the man, or the stepmother. Ask students to explain how their point of view affects the details they add or leave out.

Student Think Aloud

Use Copying Master number 6 to prompt students to share predictions made during the story and how they changed.

"I thought _____ was important in this text because _____."

Cultural Perspective

The story of Cinderella is at least 1,000 years old. Although the main character has different names, the tale has been found in North America, Scandinavia, Africa, the Middle and Far East, Asia, and around the Mediterranean. The story was first recorded in written form in the ninth century in China.

Think and Respond

1. Yeh-hsien and her stepmother treat the fish differently. What do these differences tell you about each person's character? *Possible responses: The stepmother was cruel, greedy, and dishonest. To her the fish was nothing more than food. Yeh-hsien was caring, brave, hardworking, and loyal. She treated the fish as a being worthy of respect and continued to care for it, no matter what.* **Analytical**

2. How are the characters in this fairy tale like or unlike other versions of the Cinderella story? *Possible responses: They all tell about a girl who is mistreated by a family member and whose life is changed for the better by a magical helper. Yeh-hsien includes details about Chinese culture and has its own special ending.* **Genre**

3. Why do you think fairy tales from long ago continue to be popular? *Possible responses: They carry the memory of other times, places, and people. They teach important lessons about the consequences of good and bad behavior.* **Author's Purpose**

JOHN MUIR:
MAN OF THE MOUNTAINS (1838–1914)

by Ginger Wadsworth

Genre: Biography

Text Structure: Description

Comprehension Strategy: Monitor Comprehension

Think-Aloud Copying Master number 7

Before Reading

Genre: Explain that a biography is a nonfiction selection that tells about a person's life. Tell students that a biography does not always have to be book-length to convey a vivid portrait of its subject. A good biographer can tell readers a lot about the person by focusing on a few important details. Explain that John Muir was a naturalist whose passion for California's Sierra Nevada mountains changed the course of environmental history.

Expand Vocabulary: Before reading about the life of John Muir, discuss the following words with students:

> *wiry:* thin, but very tough or strong
>
> *naturalist:* someone who studies the natural history of places
>
> *awestruck:* filled with wonder and amazement
>
> *national park system:* areas of public land across the United States that are set aside and protected by the government

Set a Purpose for Reading: Encourage students to listen to the author describe how John Muir's love of the Sierra Nevadas changed America's history.

During Reading

Use the comprehension Think Alouds during the first reading of this selection. Notes about the genre and cultural perspective may be used during subsequent readings.

JOHN MUIR:
MAN OF THE MOUNTAINS
(1838 – 1914)

by Ginger Wadsworth

"What's the quickest way out of town?" John Muir asked. In 1868, San Francisco seemed much too crowded to the wiry naturalist. He headed east, passing fields and orchards. Ahead of him stretched 400 miles of the snowcapped Sierra Nevada.

Days later, Muir reached Yosemite Valley. He saw Yosemite Falls, with a drop of more than 2,400 feet, then explored the valley which is ringed by 3,000-foot rock walls. At Mariposa Grove, he walked awestruck among the cinnamon-colored trunks of more than 600 giant sequoias, the world's largest trees. Looking east, Muir saw peaks and forested slopes. He wanted to explore everything![1]

For the rest of his life, Muir criss-crossed California's mountains again and again . . . and always on foot. Sturdy as a mountain goat, he could push through brush, leap streams, and bound from rock to rock. When it snowed, Muir walked quickly to stay warm. He smeared charcoal on his face to protect his eyes from the snow's glare. And nails sticking out of the soles of his boots helped him grip slippery ice. Once, he even climbed a tree to feel it sway in the winds during a storm.

At night, by the light of a campfire, he wrote in his journal about the animals, rivers, glaciers, and mountains he had seen. He emptied his pockets to study the plants he had collected during the day. Some nights, Muir slept on a rock in a stream to hear the water music. From his rock bed, he studied the stars and listened to the wind.

In 1871, the *New York Tribune*, a newspaper, published an article Muir had written called "Yosemite Glaciers." He published more articles, and eventually books about the beauty of the mountains. Because of his efforts, wilderness areas were set aside as parks, and John Muir is often called the father of our national park system.

Today, thousands of people hike and backpack throughout the Sierra Nevada. Like John Muir, they believe that "the mountains are calling me and I must go."[2]

Think Aloud

[1] *The way the author describes John Muir's travels through the Sierra Nevada I can visualize the peaks and slopes.*

Think Aloud

[2] *Wow! One person sure can make a difference. I notice the writer starts with one person hiking the Sierra Nevadas and ends with thousands!*

After Reading

Take Notes: Have students discuss their responses to the story, citing examples from the text to support their personal opinions.

Student Think Aloud

Use Copying Master number 7 to prompt students to choose paragraphs from the selection and tell what they were mostly about.

"This was mostly about . . ."

Cultural Perspective

Discuss the historical and cultural influences in this biography. How was the world different back then?

Think and Respond

1. Why do you think John Muir wrote about his experiences in the Sierra Nevadas? *Possible responses: He wanted to remember his experiences. He wanted to share them with others. He wanted people to help him protect the environment.* **Analytical**

2. How did the author make facts about John Muir come to life in this biography? *Possible responses: from the description of the Sierra Nevadas and other places John Muir visited, readers can imagine what his life was like.* **Text Structure**

3. What was the author's purpose? *Possible responses: The author probably wanted to show readers that John Muir's life is an example of a person who loved nature and who wanted to protect it. It might inspire them to see more of nature and to protect the environment.* **Author's Purpose**

THE SEEING STICK

a Chinese folk tale

retold by Jane Yolen

Genre: Folk Tale

Story Structure: Problem/Solution

Comprehension Strategy: Monitor Comprehension

Think-Aloud Copying Master number 6

Before Reading

Genre: Explain to students that folk tales, such as the Chinese folk tale you are about to read aloud, are as popular today as when they were first told centuries ago. A folk tale shows that people's feelings are the same no matter when or where they lived.

Expand Vocabulary: Before reading this Chinese folk tale, discuss the following words and phrases:

> *ascended the throne:* became king
>
> *effect:* to cause something to happen
>
> *flattered:* felt pleased by someone's attention
>
> *dwelt:* lived in

Set a Purpose for Reading: Ask students to listen to identify the tone, mood, and emotions in the story.

During Reading

Use the comprehension Think Alouds during the first reading of the folk tale. Notes about the genre and cultural perspective may be used during subsequent readings.

THE SEEING STICK

a Chinese folk tale
retold by Jane Yolen

Once in the ancient walled citadel of Peking
there lived an emperor who had only one daughter,
and her name was Hwei Ming.
Now this daughter had carved ivory combs
to smooth back her long black hair.
Her tiny feet were encased in embroidered slippers,
and her robes were woven of the finest silks.
But rather than making her happy,
such possessions made her sad.
For Hwei Ming was blind,
and all the beautiful handcrafts in the kingdom
brought her no pleasure at all.
Her father was also sad
that his only daughter was blind,
but he could not cry for her.
He was the emperor after all,
and had given up weeping over such things
when he ascended the throne.
Yet still he had hope
that one day Hwei Ming might be able to see.
So he resolved that if someone could help her,
such a person would be rewarded
with a fortune in jewels.
He sent word of his offer
to the inner and outer cities of Peking
and to all the towns and villages
for hundreds of miles around.[1]
Monks came, of course,
with their prayers and prayer wheels,
for they thought in this way
to help Hwei Ming see.
Magician-priests came, of course,
with their incantations and spells,
for they thought in this way
to help Hwei Ming see.
Physicians came, of course,

Think Aloud

[1] *I wonder if the problem will be solved. Maybe the emperor, with all of his riches and power, can find someone in his kingdom to help his daughter.*

with their potions and pins,
for they thought in this way
to help Hwei Ming see.
But nothing could help.
Hwei Ming had been blind from the day of her birth,
and no one could effect a cure.
Now one day
an old man, who lived far away
in the south country,
heard tales of the blind princess.
He heard of the emperor's offer.
And so he took his few possessions—
a long walking stick,
made from a single piece of golden wood,
and his whittling knife—
and started up the road.
The sun rose hot on his right side
and the sun set cool on his left
as he made his way north to Peking
to help the princess see.

At last the old man,
his clothes tattered by his travels,
stopped by the gate of the Outer City.
The guards at the gate
did not want to let such a ragged old man in.
"Grandfather, go home.
There is nothing here for such as you," they said.
The old man touched their faces in turn
with his rough fingers.
"So young," he said,
"and already so old."
He turned as if to go.
Then he propped his walking stick
against his side
and reached into his shirt
for his whittling knife.
"What are you doing, grandfather?"
called out one of the guards
when he saw the old man bring out the knife.
"I am going to show you my stick,"
said the old man.
"For it is a stick that sees."

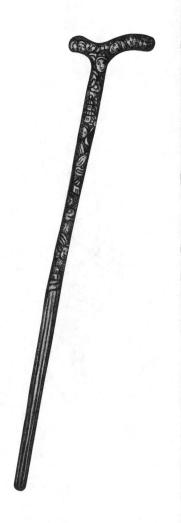

"Grandfather, that is nonsense," said the second guard.
"That stick can see no farther
than can the emperor's daughter."
"Just so, just so,"
said the old man.
"But stranger things have happened."
And so saying,
he picked up the stick
and stropped the knife blade back and forth
three times to sharpen its edge.
As the guards watched
from the gate in the wall,
the old man told them
how he had walked the many miles
through villages and towns
till he came with his seeing stick
to the walls of Peking.
And as he told them his tale,
he pointed to the pictures in the stick:
an old man,
his home,
the long walk,
the walls of Peking.
And as they watched further,
he began to cut their portraits into the wood.
The two guards looked at each other
in amazement and delight.
They were flattered at their likenesses
on the old man's stick.
Indeed, they had never witnessed such carving skill.
"Surely this is something
the guards at the wall
of the Inner City should see," they said.
So, taking the old man by the arm,
they guided him through the streets of the Outer City,
past flower peddlers and rice sellers,
past silk weavers and jewel merchants,
up to the great stone walls.
When the guards of the Inner City
saw the seeing stick,
they were surprised and delighted.
"Carve our faces, too,"

Genre Study

Folk Tale: Many folk tales include details from the country in which it was first told. In this folk tale the author describes long-ago sights of the Outer City of Peking, China.

they begged like children.
And laughing,
and touching their faces
as any fond grandfather would,
the old man did as they bid.
In no time at all, the guards of the Inner City took
the old man by his arm
and led him to the wall of the Innermost City
and in through the gate
to the great wooden doors of the Imperial Palace.
Now when the guards arrived
in the throne room of the Imperial Palace
leading the old man by the arm,
it happened that the emperor's blind daughter,
Hwei Ming,
was sitting by his side,
her hands clasped before her,
silent, sightless, and still.
As the guards finished telling
of the wonderful pictures carved on the golden stick,
the princess clapped her hands.

"Oh, I wish I could see that wondrous stick," she said.
"Just so, just so," said the old man.
"And I will show it to you.
For it is no ordinary piece of wood,
but a stick that sees."
"What nonsense," said her father
in voice so low it was almost a growl.
But the princess did not hear him.
She had already bent toward
the sound of the old man's voice.
"A seeing stick?"
The old man did not say anything for a moment.
Then he leaned forward
and petted Hwei Ming's head
and caressed her cheek.
For though she was a princess,
she was still a child.
Then the old man began to tell again
the story of his long journey to Peking.
He introduced each character and object—
the old man,

the guards,
the great walls,
the Innermost City.
And then he carved the wooden doors,
the Imperial Palace,
the princess, into the golden wood.
When he finished,
the old man reached out
for the princess's small hands.
He took her tiny fingers in his
and placed them on the stick.
Finger on finger,
he helped her trace the likenesses.
"Feel the long flowing hair of the princess,"
the old man said.
"Grown as she herself has grown,
straight and true."
And Hwei Ming touched the carved stick.
"Now feel your own long hair," he said.
And she did.
"Feel the lines in the old man's face," he said.
"From years of worry and years of joy."
He thrust the stick into her hands again.
And the princess' slim fingers
felt the carved stick.
Then he put her fingers onto his face
and traced the same lines there.
It was the first time
the princess had touched another person's face
since she was a very small girl.
The princess jumped up from her throne
and thrust her hands before her.
"Guards, O guards," she cried out.
"Come here to me."
And the guards lifted up their faces
to the Princess Hwei Ming's hands.
Her fingers,
like little breezes,
brushed their eyes and noses and mouths,
and then found each one on the carved stick.
Hwei Ming turned to her father,
the emperor,

who sat straight and tall
and unmoving on his great throne.
She reached out
and her fingers ran eagerly
through his hair
and down his nose and cheek
and rested curiously on a tear they found there.[2]
And that was strange, indeed,
for had not the emperor
given up crying over such things
when he ascended the throne?
They brought her
through the streets of the city, then,
the emperor in the lead.
And Princess Hwei Ming
touched men and women
and children as they passed.
Till at last
she stood before the great walls of Peking
and felt the stones themselves.
Then she turned to the old man.
Her voice was bright
and full of laughter.
"Tell me another tale," she said.
"Tomorrow, if you wish," he replied.
For each tomorrow
as long as he lived,
the old man <u>dwelt</u>
in the Innermost City,
where only the royal family stays.
The emperor rewarded him
with a fortune in jewels,
but the old man gave them all away.
Every day
he told the princess a story.
Some were tales as ancient
as the city itself.
Some were as new
as the events of the day.
And each time
he carved wonderful images
in the stick of golden wood.[3]

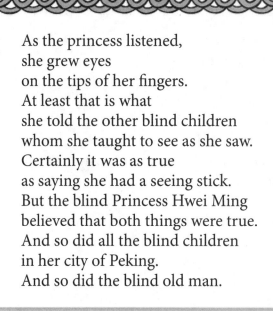

As the princess listened,
she grew eyes
on the tips of her fingers.
At least that is what
she told the other blind children
whom she taught to see as she saw.
Certainly it was as true
as saying she had a seeing stick.
But the blind Princess Hwei Ming
believed that both things were true.
And so did all the blind children
in her city of Peking.
And so did the blind old man.

 **After Reading**

Retell the Story: Have students tell the story as if they were the emperor, the old man, or Princess Hwei Ming. Encourage students to share what they, as the character, are feeling at different points in the story. Have them also include mood and tone.

Student Think Aloud

Use Copying Master number 6 to prompt students to tell about a prediction they made while reading the story and how that prediction changed.

"I thought _____ was important because _____."

Cultural Perspective

Have the students identify all the cultural, historical, and social aspects or influences in the story. Then ask them to identify any recurring themes, patterns, symbols and to compare this folk tale with others they might have read from other cultures.

Think and Respond

1. How does the princess "grow eyes on the ends of her fingers"? How does the old man help her do this? *Possible responses: Her fingers become her eyes because she can trace people's faces and create a picture of them in her mind. The old man shows her how to touch different things and recognize the pictures that he creates in his seeing stick.* **Analytical**

2. Why do you think so many people around the world enjoy folk tales? *Possible responses: Just like the princess, people like to use their imaginations to picture things they have not seen with their own eyes. They relate to the characters because they have the same hopes and feelings.* **Genre**

3. How does the author give clues that point to the old man's blindness? Name some. *Possible responses: She has him carry a stick while walking across China. Some blind people also carry sticks that help them navigate around things. She also says he touches the guards' faces before carving in his stick. He touches Hwei Ming's face before carving it.* **Author's Purpose**

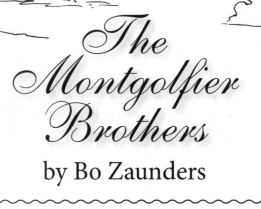

The Montgolfier Brothers
by Bo Zaunders

Genre: Narrative Nonfiction

Text Structure: Description

Comprehension Strategy: Monitor Comprehension

Think-Aloud Copying Master number 3

Before Reading

Genre: Tell students that you are going to read aloud a narrative nonfiction selection about the invention of the hot-air balloon. Remind students that in narrative nonfiction, the author uses facts to tell a story. The author may add details such as dialogue and descriptions to the story to make it more interesting. Invite students to recall other narrative nonfiction selections they have heard, such as "Close Encounters of the Bear Kind" and "Barry: The Dog Who Saved People."

Expand Vocabulary: Before reading, introduce the following words and terms:

> *jostling:* pushing and shoving
>
> *menagerie:* a collection of various animals
>
> *perplexing:* puzzling or confusing
>
> *physics:* the scientific study of matter, energy, force, and motion
>
> *ruminating:* thinking deeply about something

Set a Purpose for Reading: Suggest that students listen to find out how the Montgolfier brothers invented the hot-air balloon.

During Reading

Use the comprehension Think Alouds during the first reading of the selection. Notes about the genre may be used during subsequent readings.

The Montgolfier Brothers

by Bo Zaunders

Everyone at Louis XVI's magnificent château in Versailles clamored for a good view. Spectators crammed the windows and filled the rooftops. In the courtyard below, amidst the milling, jostling crowd, a huge, multicolored cloth stirred and rose, apparently on its own. It was September 19, 1783. Some 130,000 people watched with excitement as the first free-flying, hot-air balloon ever to carry living creatures was about to be launched. The passengers: a sheep, a duck, and a rooster.

Off it went, this small menagerie. The king, as curious as anyone, watched the flight through field glasses. When the balloon came down just two miles away, he turned to one of its inventors, Étienne Montgolfier, and said, "*Magnifique!* But now we must find out if the animals survived."[1]

When picked up by the king's men, the sheep, duck, and rooster proved to be in excellent condition. In a letter to his wife that evening, an exultant Étienne playfully quoted the three as saying, "We feel fine. We've landed safely despite the wind. It's given us an appetite." In his own voice, Étienne continued, "That is all we could gather from the talk of the three travelers, seeing that they don't know how to write and that we have neglected to teach them French. The first could say only '*Quack, Quack*'; the second, '*Cock-a-doodle-do*'; and the third, no doubt a member of the Lamb family, replied only '*Baa*' to all our questions."

It had been a long, exciting day. Before drifting off to sleep, a happy Étienne chuckled to himself as he recalled his brother Joseph-Michel's reaction to the choice of animal passengers. "Try to take a cow," he had written. "That will create an extra–ordinary effect, far more than a panicky sheep that no one will be able to see." Dear old Joseph. It was he who had started it all with that urgent and rather perplexing note ten months ago . . .

Back then, Étienne lived in the small town of Annonay in southern France, managing the family's papermaking factory. Joseph, older by five years, lived in a neighboring city, Avignon, where he spent most of his time reading books on physics and conducting experiments. An amateur scientist, Joseph had been ruminating in front of his fireplace one evening, questioning

Genre Study

Narrative Nonfiction: Narrative nonfiction often tells details about a topic in the order in which they happened. But to make a selection more interesting, the writer can use a flashback. This selection begins with an exciting event and then switches back to a past event. In this way, the writer explains how the invention got to this point in time.

Think Aloud

[1] *The word* magnifique *must be French. It looks like the word* magnificent, *so I predict that it means something similar. The word* magnificent *would make sense as an interjection in the context of this sentence.*

Think Aloud

[2] I made a connection when the author described how Joseph watches the fire in his fireplace. I have also noticed how smoke, small bits of ash, and sparks rise up into the chimney. No wonder he had the idea for a hot-air balloon.

whether the "gas" that whisked the smoke, sparks, and pieces of charred paper up the chimney could be made to lift solid, man-made objects.[2] Anxious to find out, he set to work right there in the room, constructing a lightweight, boxlike frame of thin wooden slats. Around it he stretched silk taffeta, leaving a one-foot-square opening at the bottom. Resting the box on a support, he inserted scraps of paper through the opening and ignited them. In seconds, the contraption rose and bumped against the ceiling—dumbfounding his landlady, who happened to be present. Excited, Joseph dashed off a note to his favorite younger brother: "Get in a supply of taffeta and cordage, quickly, and you'll see one of the most astonishing sights in the world."

A few days later in a field outside Annonay, with Étienne as an enthusiastic audience, Joseph launched yet another "little box," which soared to seventy feet and floated in the air for a full minute. Together the brothers built larger models, modifying the original design to the spherical shape of a classical balloon.

On June 5, after much experimentation, they staged a public demonstration with a balloon made of coarsely woven fabric layered with paper. As the hot air from a small fire filled the limp bag, it swelled into a bulging globe, thirty-five feet wide, and, to the townspeople's utter amazement, shot straight into the sky. It ascended to a height of a thousand feet and rode on the air currents for over a mile.

Word of the demonstration reached Paris, where a scientist, J. A. C. Charles, soon developed a different kind of balloon, using hydrogen gas instead of hot air. On account of his successful launch of a much smaller balloon—eighteen feet in diameter—and the June 5 launch of the Montgolfier brothers, balloons became the hot topic throughout the country. Particularly

impressed by the Montgolfier accomplishment, the king ordered a command performance at Versailles—the one that would launch the sheep, the duck, and the rooster.

Only Étienne should go, the family decided. Joseph was too shy and unworldly for such an important mission. Before Étienne left, their father, predicting that human flight would come next, made one condition: His sons must swear an oath never to fly any of their perilous machines themselves. That would be left for two other men to do—in Paris on November 21, 1783.

All Paris came out to watch this Montgolfier balloon—seven stories high and decorated with golden suns, the signs of the zodiac, and the king's monogram. The king doubted that people would survive balloon flight, so he suggested that two criminals under sentence of death be used for the experiment. Pilâtre de Rozier, a young scientist, protested vehemently. Why should, as he put it, "two vile criminals have the first glory of rising to the sky?" He volunteered, along with his aristocratic friend, Marquis d'Arlandes.

Up went this incredible object. It was a fearsome sight; many were on their knees, praying. As a hushed silence prevailed throughout the city, the voices of the two airborne voyagers could be heard quite clearly. Stationed on a circular platform at the bottom of the balloon, they joked and shouted commands at each other as they forked bundles of straw into the balloon's burner. A moment of panic! Sparks from the flames began eating holes in the fabric of their fragile craft. But the men were prepared—with buckets of water and sponges attached to long poles. Minutes later they were nearly skewered on a church tower. The flight lasted about twenty minutes. On landing, Pilâtre's coat caught fire. Fortunately, he wasn't wearing it.[3]

Think Aloud

[3] *Wow! I am able to picture in my mind what it was like in Paris that day, almost as if I were watching it as news on television. From the people praying, the fires, and nearly getting stuck on the tower, it must have been scary and exciting.*

After Reading

Take Notes: Ask students to take notes of important events that occur in the selection. Then ask students to work with a partner to list the events in sequence.

Student Think Aloud

Use Copying Master number 3 to prompt students to tell what they pictured as they read certain details in the selection.

"I was able to picture in my mind . . ."

Cultural Perspectives

Have the students discuss all the historical, social, and cultural elements and aspects of this folk tale, giving examples from the text. Ask students to identify how the setting, events, vocabulary, and characters' perspectives are specific to the historic era and culture. Then have students consider: If this story took place in modern times, how would it be different?

Think and Respond

1. Who first had the idea for the hot-air balloon, and what inspired him? What does that tell you about inspiration? *Possible responses: Joseph, the older brother, was watching the fireplace and noticed that something lifted the smoke, sparks, and paper up out of the chimney. He wondered if it could also lift a balloon made of cloth. This shows that you never know where inspiration will come from.* **Analytical**

2. The writer starts with a description of the experimental flight in September of 1783 and then tells in flashback something that happened ten months earlier. Why do you think that is? *Possible response: to gain readers' interest with a very exciting event and then explain what led up to it* **Text Structure**

3. Why do you think the author includes parts of letters written between the two brothers and other relatives? *Possible response: The author wants to give more interesting information about the brothers, especially what they were thinking and feeling.* **Author's Purpose**

The Microscope

by Maxine Kumin

Genre: Poem

Poetic Element: Rhyme and Rhythm

Comprehension Strategy: Summarize

Think-Aloud Copying Master number 7

 Before Reading

Genre: Tell students that the poem you are going to read aloud has a rhyme scheme, or rhyme pattern. The poet creates a rhyme pattern with different ending words in each line. Explain that this poem is about Anton Leeuwenhoek (pronounced LAY-ven-hook), the inventor of the microscope.

Expand Vocabulary: Before reading aloud the poem about scientist Anton Leeuwenhoek, review the following words and phrases with students:

> *fumed:* felt angry
>
> *dry goods:* fabric, clothing, and other products that do not include hardware or food
>
> *tending store:* taking care of or managing a store
>
> *lenses:* pieces of curved and polished glass that form an image when light passes through them

Set a Purpose for Reading: Ask students to listen for alliteration and consonance in the poem.

 **During Reading**

For the first reading, read the poem all the way through, emphasizing the rhyming pairs in each verse. On subsequent readings, discuss the comprehension Think Aloud and genre note.

The Microscope

by Maxine Kumin

Anton Leeuwenhoek was Dutch.
He sold pincushions, cloth, and such.
The waiting townsfolk fumed and fussed
As Anton's dry goods gathered dust.

He worked, instead of tending store,
At grinding special lenses for
A microscope. Some of the things
He looked at were:

          mosquitoes' wings,
the hairs of sheep, the legs of lice,
the skin of people, dogs, and mice;
ox eyes, spiders' spinning gear,
fishes' scales, a little smear
of his own blood,
          and best of all,
the unknown, busy, very small
bugs that swim and bump and hop
inside a simple water drop.[1]

Impossible! most Dutchmen said.
This Anton's crazy in the head.
We ought to ship him off to Spain.
He says he's seen a housefly's brain.
He says the water that we drink
Is full of bugs. He's mad, we think!

They called him *dummkopf*, which means dope.
That's how we got the microscope.

After Reading

Set a Purpose for Rereading: Reread the poem and ask students to give examples of alliteration, the repetition of beginning consonant sounds; and consonance, the repetition of consonant sounds in the middle or end of words. Then ask students to paraphrase the poem.

Student Think Aloud

Use Copying Master number 7 to prompt students to choose sections of the poem and discuss what they were mostly about. Then have students identify author bias and perspective.

"This was mostly about…"

Think and Respond

1. Why did some people think that Anton was a *dummkopf*? What was he really doing when he invented the microscope? *Possible responses: People did not understand the science behind what he was doing. When he saw "bugs" in a drop of water, people thought he must be imagining it because they were too small to be seen by the naked eye. He was learning what living things are made of by seeing them greatly magnified.* **Analytical**

2. What are some of the rhyme schemes in the poem? *Possible responses: The first and fourth verses are* aabb, *the second verse is* aabc, *the third verse is* abbccd, *the fifth verse is* aabbcc, *and the sixth verse is* aa. **Genre**

3. Why do you think the poet wrote this poem? *Possible responses: She tells about an important scientific discovery in an entertaining and memorable way. She shows that both scientists and poets look for patterns in things.* **Author's Purpose**

Plays and Choral Readings

It Couldn't Be Done

by Edgar A. Guest

Group 1: Somebody said that it couldn't be done,
But he with a chuckle replied
That "maybe it couldn't," but he would be one
Who wouldn't say so till he'd tried.
So he buckled right in with the trace of a grin
On his face. If he worried he hid it.

All: He started to sing as he tackled the thing
That couldn't be done, and he did it.

Group 2: Somebody scoffed: "Oh, you'll never do that;
At least no one ever has done it";
But he took off his coat and he took off his hat,
And the first thing we knew he'd begun it.
With a lift of his chin and a bit of a grin,
Without any doubting or quiddit,

All: He started to sing as he tackled the thing
That couldn't be done, and he did it.

Group 3: There are thousands to tell you it cannot be done,
There are thousands to prophesy failure;
There are thousands to point out to you, one by one,
The dangers that wait to assail you.
But just buckle in with a bit of a grin,
Just take off your coat and go to it;

All: Just start to sing as you tackle the thing
That "cannot be done," and you'll do it.

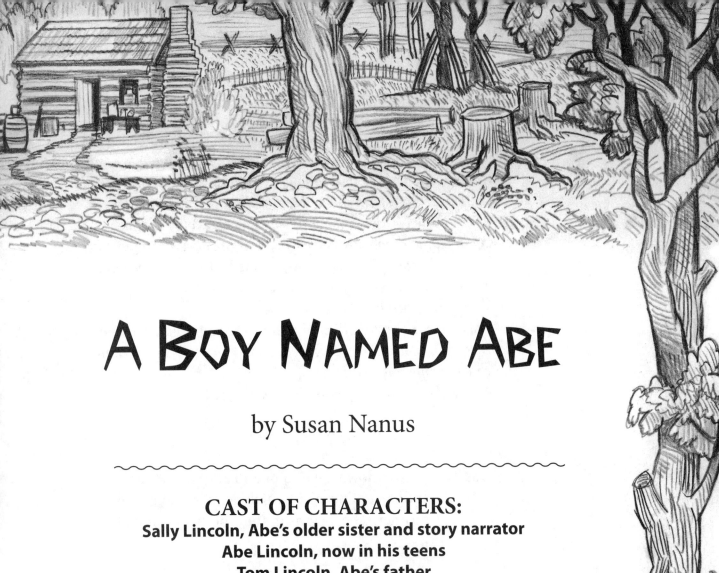

A Boy Named Abe

by Susan Nanus

CAST OF CHARACTERS:

Sally Lincoln, Abe's older sister and story narrator
Abe Lincoln, now in his teens
Tom Lincoln, Abe's father
Nathaniel Brown, a wealthy neighbor
Josiah Crawford, a farmer
Mrs. Crawford, a farmer
Dennis Hanks, Abe's cousin
James Taylor, a storekeeper
Mrs. Taylor, a storekeeper
Gentleman
John Dill, a ferryman
Martha Dill, John's wife and partner in the ferry business
Squire Samuel Pate, a justice of the peace

TIME:
the 1820s

SETTING:
Pigeon Creek, Indiana

Abraham Lincoln, the sixteenth President of the United States, was born in a log cabin in the woods of Kentucky. When he was seven his family moved to Indiana. Always an eager student, young Abe loved to spend his time reading. Later in life he became a lawyer. He served a term in Congress and was elected President in 1860. The Civil War was fought during Lincoln's term of office, and he had the difficult job of seeing our country through the bloodiest period in its history. The play A Boy Named Abe *shows the kind of strengths the young Lincoln had as a child. Which of these qualities do you think helped him to become a leader?*

The almost-bare stage divides into two sections: indoor scenes, stage right; outdoor scenes, stage left. Signs can be set up on chairs to indicate the different locations.

Abe is sitting cross-legged in the woods, reading.

~~~~~~

Sally: [enters downstage right and addresses the audience] Our play, which is mainly about my brother, Abe, begins in the woods by our cabin.

[Tom Lincoln enters.]

Tom: [calling out] Abe! Abe Lincoln, where are you?

Sally: [to the audience] That's my brother Abe over there reading. He's always getting in trouble because he loves books so much.

Tom: [finding Abe reading] There are a hundred things to do, and I won't have you wasting time!

[Nathaniel Brown, a well-dressed man, enters stage left.]

Nathaniel: Tom Lincoln?

Tom: Mr. Brown, what are you doing here?

Nathaniel: Your wife said I could find you out here in the woods. [He pulls out a paper from his coat.] I have the deed right here.

Abe: Deed?

Tom: Mr. Brown is going to buy some land behind the cabin. Eighteen acres to be exact. Right, Mr. Brown?

Nathaniel: That's right, Tom. Now, I brought a pen and some ink, so if you'll just sign your name. . . . [He pulls out a quill pen and a little bottle of ink.]

Abe: Uh, Pa—would you like me to read the deed?

Nathaniel: There's no need for you to read it. Everything is in perfect order.

Abe: You shouldn't sign something without knowing what's in it, Pa.

Tom: Hmm. You may be right. Okay. Take a look.

[Tom hands the deed to Abe, who begins to read. Tom leans to look at the deed. Nathaniel Brown sneaks away, stage left.]

Abe: Just what I thought.

Tom: What?

Abe: If you sign this, Pa, he'll get the whole farm.

Tom: What! You mean he tried to cheat me? Why, you . . . [He looks around, sees that Nathaniel is gone.] Well, Abe, looks like for once your reading came in pretty handy.

Sally: After that, Pa doesn't bother Abe so much about his reading. A couple of years go by. Abe is the tallest, strongest boy in Pigeon Creek. Now other folks pay to have him work on their farms. This is what happens in the Crawfords' kitchen.

[The Crawfords enter. Josiah has an account book and pen. Mrs. Crawford begins to make an apple pie. Abe enters stage right.]

Josiah: Well, Abe, you've been both a farmhand and carpenter this week. You plowed and planted the back field, repaired the barn roof, and built a new fence. I guess I owe you a pretty penny for all that.

Abe: Yes, sir.

Mrs. Crawford: If you'll wait a while, I'll have some fresh-baked apple pie for you.

Abe: Thanks, Mrs. Crawford, but I better get home. Only . . .

Josiah: Well, what is it, boy? Speak up.

Abe: I was wondering . . . if you don't mind . . . if I could maybe borrow one of those books? [He points to an imaginary bookshelf.]

Josiah: You hear that, Mrs. Crawford? Abe prefers a book to a piece of your pie!

Abe: Oh, I'm sorry, I didn't mean . . .

Mrs. Crawford: Nonsense, Abe. I know what you meant. And you just help yourself to any book on that shelf.

Abe: Thank you! [He approaches the shelf and reads the titles.] I think I'll take *The Life of George Washington* by Mason Weems. [He takes the book from the shelf gently.] I really want to study him.

Josiah: Abe, with all this studying, you'll go far. Maybe as far as Washington! [He laughs at his joke.]

Mrs. Crawford: Oh, Josiah! That really wasn't funny! [The Crawfords exit stage right, as Abe starts reading.]

Sally: [setting up 'The Lincolns' Cabin' sign] That night, Abe stays up half the night, reading his new book.

[As Sally speaks, Abe closes the book and puts it in a crack in the wall between two imaginary logs. Then Abe gets into bed and falls asleep.]

Sally: Abe sleeps in the loft. There's a big storm. Rain drips through the cracks and . . . the book is ruined! Our cousin Dennis finds Abe the next day.

[Dennis enters stage right and walks to Abe.]

Dennis: What's the matter? You sick or something?

Abe: Look what happened to Mr. Crawford's book! I don't believe it! It's all wet and wrinkled from the rain.

Dennis: Oh, boy! You're in for it now. What will you say? The cabin burned down? A robber stole it?

Abe: I'd sure like to have an excuse, but I don't. I guess I'll just have to tell Mr. Crawford the truth.

Dennis: Old Honest Abe, huh, boy?

Abe: I guess so, Dennis.

Sally: So Abe goes and tells Mr. Crawford just what happened. [As she speaks, Josiah Crawford enters.]

Josiah: That book cost a lot of money, Abe.

Abe: I know, sir.

Josiah: And money doesn't grow on trees.

Abe: I know, sir.

Josiah: Lending you the book was generous on my part.

Abe: Indeed it was, sir.

Josiah: It was your responsibility to take good care of it.

Abe: [looking down] Yes, sir.

Josiah: Well, it was an accident. But you can work off the cost. Three days in the fields should do it.

Abe: [gratefully] Yes, sir. And . . . here's the book. [He holds it out.] You can still read the pages inside.

Josiah: You want it? You can have it. As long as you don't read it on the job. Now, get to work!

Abe: Yes, Mr. Crawford. And thank you. Thank you so much!

[Josiah and the others clear the chairs, leaving the table as a store counter. Josiah exits stage right as the Taylors enter and stand on one side of the counter, Abe on the other.]

Sally: In 1825, Abe is 16. He helps the Taylors run their store. The store is at Posey's Landing on the bank of Andersen's Creek, close to the Ohio River. Steamboats go up and down the Ohio, and there's a ferry that takes folks from here to the other side of the river, where the boats dock. The Taylors are about to leave on a trip.

James: Now remember, Abe. The beans are over there and the flour is in the back.

Mrs. Taylor: We don't give credit, remember that.

Abe: Yes, ma'am.

James: [pointing] Nails and other hardware over here.

Mrs. Taylor: No money, no merchandise.

Abe: Yes, Mrs. Taylor.

James: [nodding toward an imaginary shelf] Cloth and dress patterns on the shelf.

Abe: You know, it's getting late.

James: He's right! Come on, Mrs. Taylor, we've a coach to catch, and the driver doesn't plan to wait for us.

[James takes her arm, and they exit.]

Abe: [goes to the door and peers in both directions] No customers in sight, so . . . [He pulls a book from his pocket and begins to read.]

A gentleman rushes into the store.

Gentleman: [with agitation] Quick! That rowboat outside. Whose is it?

Abe: Well, it's mine, but—

Gentleman: I'll give you two dollars to row me out to the steamboat right now.

Abe: Well . . . okay. Let's go.

[The two rush stage left to an imaginary rowboat. Abe pantomimes rowing it.]

Sally: But what Abe thinks is a good deed almost gets him into trouble.

[The Dills enter stage left and stand, on the riverbank, watching as Abe approaches.]

Sally: The Dills own the ferry that takes passengers from the shore across the river to where the boats dock.

John: [showing disbelief] Do you see what I see, Martha?

Martha: How dare he! Who is he?

John: It's Abe Lincoln. The Pigeon Creek boy who works for the Taylors. He could steal our business, Martha.

[Midstream, the gentleman climbs out of the rowboat and onto the steamboat and exits stage left. Abe starts rowing back to the store.]

John: Hey, you! Abe Lincoln!

Martha: Come over here a minute, will you?

Abe: What for?

[Abe reverses direction and rows toward the Dills.]

John: Don't you know you can't ferry people across the river without a license? You've broken the law!

Martha: We have a license, and you don't!

John: You're coming with us, young man!

Martha: If the Justice of the Peace finds you guilty, you'll be thrown in jail!

[Martha takes one of Abe's arms; John takes the other. They half-lead, half-pull him stage right as Squire Samuel Pate, carrying his gavel, enters the courtroom from stage right.]

Sally: And that is how Abe comes to meet Squire Samuel Pate, Justice of the Peace, who is holding forth right now.

Squire Pate: Order! Order in the court. State your case.

John: Your Honor, Martha and I have a license to ferry passengers across the river. And we caught this boy red-handed rowing a man to the steamboat.

Squire Pate: [to Abe] What do you say to that, young man?

Abe: What he says is true. But their license is to carry folks across the river. I only went to the middle. So I don't think I really broke the law.

Squire Pate: [pulling out a thick book and leafing through it] The law is plain. You two have the right to set a person across, but there's no law against rowing passengers to midstream.

John: What! But that's not fair!

Squire Pate: [banging his gavel] Quiet! Case closed.

[John and Martha storm out stage left.]

Squire Pate: You've got a good head on your shoulders, young man. What's your name?

Abe: Abraham Lincoln, sir. I'm interested in the law.

Squire Pate: Then you should read this book. Knowing the law of the land never hurts.

[Abe takes the book reverently.]

Squire Pate: Would you like to come to my court and listen in sometime?

Abe: You would let me do that, Your Honor?

Squire Pate: Yes I would. I believe you want to learn. And I'd not be surprised if you want to do something big with what you learn. Am I right?

Abe: I hope I can, sir. I will surely try.

Squire Pate: Young man, I expect great things of you.

Sally: And that's how Abe took his first step toward being a lawyer and after that a congressman and after that . . . well, you already know. Abe was always determined to learn and to do something good with what he learned. Thank you, Squire Pate, for helping Abe take that first important step.

There are many stories told about Abraham Lincoln's youth. Some might be true, some might be made up, but all are entertaining. The writer of this play chose a few stories that she had read about Abraham Lincoln and dramatized them—or made them into scenes in a play. If you wanted to do the same, how could you find additional stories about Lincoln's life to dramatize? What kind of story do you think would make a good scene?

A Thousand Miles to Freedom

CAST:

Narrator
William Craft
Ellen Craft
Ticket Seller
Conductor 1
Mr. Cray
Driver
Passenger
Captain 1

Slave Buyer
Pompey
Ticket Agent
Captain 2
Woman
Conductor 2
Station Master
Onlooker

Sunday, December 17, 1848
Macon, Georgia

Narrator: It was a still December night in the year 1848. On the grounds of a fine plantation in Macon, Georgia, a light burned in a small cabin near the main house. Inside, a young couple talked. Ellen Craft gave every appearance of being white, with her fair skin and straight hair, so like her father. However, as the daughter of a black woman, she was obliged by law to follow her mother's condition. And so she was as much a slave as her mother—and as her husband, William Craft. As the couple spoke, their voices were hushed, not due to the lateness of the hour, but rather to the subject of their discussion.

William: Ellen, listen! I got a plan, and I think it'll work!

Ellen: A plan for our escape, William? What is it? Tell me!

William: You'll pretend to be white, and I'll travel with you as your manservant. You'll dress yourself up as a young white gentleman—a sickly gentleman needing help. We'll take the train north, to Philadelphia and freedom!

Ellen: Oh, William, we don't dare! Pretending to be white would be hard enough, but I could never act the part of a white gentleman for a journey of a thousand miles.

William: Ellen, listen to me. Think of what'll happen if we don't dare. We'll belong to our masters forever—slaves to be bought and sold.

Ellen: I think of nothing else! If we had children, they'd be the master's property, too. They could be torn away from us at any time. I could not bear it! . . . you're right, William. We must dare. Let us get the things we need for the disguise. I will try to carry out the plan.

Narrator: William Craft was what was called a town slave. Trained in woodworking, his master hired him out to a cabinetmaker, a Mr. John Knight. William's wages went to his master, but he was allowed to keep the money that he made by working overtime. It was with these savings that the couple planned to finance their flight to freedom. Over the next few days, William went to different parts of town at odd times to purchase the articles they needed: a coat, a shirt, a hat, boots, and a pair of dark-green spectacles for Ellen. He couldn't find trousers small enough, so Ellen carefully stitched them herself. At last, the disguise was assembled.

William: We're ready. All that needs doing is to get visiting passes for a few days over Christmas. Most likely your mistress won't refuse—with you being her favorite slave and all.

Ellen: I'll say I want to visit my dying old aunt for Christmas.

William: And I'll ask Mr. Knight if I can go with you. He's a mighty suspicious man, but since I've never asked for a pass before, maybe he'll say yes. . . . If no one 'spects us back till after Christmas, they won't be looking for us till we're safe in Philadelphia. I surely pray we get those passes.

Narrator: The next day, William returned to the cabin with the precious paper in his pocket. He showed it to Ellen.

Ellen: And here is mine!

William: It's a wonder, Ellen. These papers are life or death to us, and we can't even read 'em.

Ellen: Cannot read. . . . Oh, William, our plan will never work. I just remembered something I heard my mistress say. Travelers must write their names in a book when staying in a hotel, as well as at the Custom House in Charleston, South Carolina. And I can neither read nor write my name. We are lost, William, we are lost!

Narrator: Sitting in their little room that night, Ellen and William were on the verge of despair. All at once, Ellen raised her head, a smile replacing her tears.

Ellen: William, it has come to me. You'll bandage my right hand and bind it up in a sling. Then it would seem right for me to ask someone at the hotel to write my name for me!

William: Yes! That'll do it!

Ellen: Perhaps, too, I should bind some herb poultices under my chin with strips of cloth. The bandages will add to my sickly appearance and hide the fact that I have no beard.

William: We'll make you look like you're sufferin' from a mighty bad toothache!

Narrator: William and Ellen worked all through the night reviewing their plans and making their preparations. As a personal maid in the big house, Ellen had learned much. Though she could not read or write, she was as well-spoken as her mistress. As a house servant, she often overheard conversations about trips up North. She had stored in her mind information that might someday prove helpful to her and to William. Now that day had finally come.

Thursday, December 21, 1848
From Macon, Georgia to Savannah, Georgia

Narrator: Shortly before dawn, William cut Ellen's hair. Then he helped her on with the disguise.

William: Hold still while I fasten this bow tie. You surely do make a most respectable gentleman. People'd never guess a slave is hiding behind those spectacles and bandages.

Ellen: I hope you're right, William. I fear the next few days may be worse than the twenty-two years I've spent as a slave.

William: It's time to blow the candle out now. Hold my hand, and let us pray for success. Think of it—freedom for Christmas!

Narrator: A few moments later, they rose and stood together in breathless silence. What if someone had been about the cabin listening and watching their movements? William took his wife by the hand, stepped to the door, drew it open, and peeped out. Though there were trees surrounding the cabin, the foliage scarcely moved. In fact, everything appeared to be as still as death.

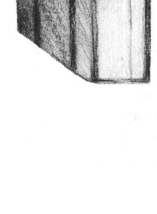

William: [whispering] Come, my dear. I will latch the door behind us one last time.

Ellen: Now that the hour has finally come, I am so afraid.

William: Me, too, Ellen. I've never been so scared, Every inch of this thousand miles seems like a mountain. But we've got to go on! There's no turning back now!

Narrator: They stepped out as softly as moonlight upon the water and tiptoed cautiously across the yard into the street. They scarcely breathed for fear of waking the sleeping household.

William: This is where I leave you, Ellen, for we cannot be seen together in Macon. Do you remember what you must do?

Ellen: Yes. From this moment, I must act as Mr. William Johnson, on my way to Philadelphia to seek medical advice. My slave, William, is along to attend me. I will go to the train station now and buy our tickets to Savannah, Georgia.

William: And I'll board the last car with the other slaves. I'll look for you on the platform in Savannah.

Narrator: They walked separately, in different directions, to the railway station. Ellen felt both excitement and fear. Pretending to be free, she suddenly felt free—but

real freedom was still a thousand miles away. As she walked into the red-brick station, she reminded herself of all the gestures a young, white gentleman might use—flicking lint from a coat lapel or hooking his thumbs in his vest pockets. Then she squared her shoulders and walked up to the ticket window.

Ellen: Two tickets to Savannah, please. One for myself and one for my slave.

Ticket Seller: Here you are, sir. Have a pleasant journey.

Ellen: I thank you kindly, sir.

Conductor 1: A-l-l aboard!

Narrator: From his seat in the car at the end of the train, William watched Ellen board one of the front carriages. Then, in amazement and horror, he saw Mr. Knight, the cabinetmaker for whom he worked, rush across the train platform. He began looking suspiciously at the passengers in each of the carriages.

William: It's Mr. Knight! Why would he be looking for me so soon?

Narrator: Mr. Knight moved from one car to another, coming closer and closer to where William sat. With a pounding heart, William shrank into a corner and turned his face away from the door.

Conductor 1: A-l-l aboard!

Narrator: William expected to be grabbed from his seat at any moment. Suddenly, the train's whistle blew and the wheels began to turn. Mr. Knight jumped down from the train onto the platform as the train began to pick up speed. Only then did William sit up in his seat and begin to breathe more freely. But he might not have breathed quite so freely had he known that at this very moment, in another carriage, "Mr. Johnson" was also facing a fearful encounter.

Mr. Cray: It's a very fine morning, sir.

Narrator: It was Mr. Cray speaking. He was a friend of Ellen's master, and he had taken a seat next to "Mr. Johnson"! Fearful that Mr. Cray might recognize her voice, Ellen pretended not to hear.

Mr. Cray: [in a louder voice] It's a very fine morning, sir.

Narrator: Again, he did not receive an answer.

Mr. Cray: I will make him hear! [loudly] It's a very fine morning, sir!

Ellen: Yes . . . yes, it is.

Mr. Cray: Poor fellow, he must be deaf. I shall not trouble him anymore.

Narrator: "Mr. Johnson" breathed a little easier, but was very glad when Mr. Cray got off the train several stops later. Finally, as evening fell, the train pulled into the Savannah station. "Mr. Johnson" stepped down off the train and saw William waiting on the platform.

William: You must find a carriage, master. I'll follow behind with the bags.

Ellen: Of course, William. There's a carriage at the station entrance. We'll take it.

Driver: Might you be going to the Charleston steamer, sir?

Ellen: Yes, I am.

Driver: Right this way, then. Let me help you, sir. I can see that you are not well. Your slave can ride up on top.

Ellen: I thank you, sir.

Narrator: The carriage took William and Ellen through the streets of Savannah to the steamer bound for Charleston, South Carolina. Soon after boarding, "Mr. Johnson" retired to his cabin to avoid encountering the other passengers. William followed behind with the bags. The minute the door shut behind them, Ellen pulled off her spectacles and hugged her husband.

© Macmillan/McGraw-Hill

Ellen: Oh, William, what a trial. When Mr. Cray sat down beside me, it was all I could do to keep myself from jumping off that train! But we did it, William. They believed me!

William: I was sure we'd be caught when I saw old Mr. Knight come looking through the carriages. But as neither man recognized you, I do believe we've got a chance!

Ellen: William, did you hear the others talking as we boarded? They think it odd that I retired so early. Perhaps you had better warm some flannel cloths and liniment by the stove where all are sure to notice you.

William: The smell alone will make it mighty clear you're ill.

Narrator: The passengers certainly did take notice of William.

Passenger: What is that you've got there?

William: Opodeldoc liniment, sir, for my master's rheumatism.

Passenger: It stinks enough to kill or cure twenty men! Away with it, or I reckon I'll throw it overboard!

Narrator: Satisfied that he had accomplished his purpose, William took the cloths and the opodeldoc back to his master's cabin. He waited a few minutes and then went back on deck, where he met the ship's captain.

William: Begging your pardon, sir. Where do slaves sleep, sir?

Captain 1: Slaves? We have no sleeping accommodations set aside for your kind on this ship. You can sleep standing up for all I care!

Narrator: So William paced the deck for several hours, and then found some cotton sacks in a warm spot near the funnel. He dozed there, waiting for morning, when he would assist his master in preparing for breakfast.

Friday, December 22, 1848
From Charleston, South Carolina to Wilmington,
North Carolina

Narrator: At breakfast, "Mr. Johnson" was seated beside the captain in the ship's dining room.

Captain 1: Good morning, sir. How are you feeling today?

Passenger: I do hope your rheumatism is improved this morning?

Ellen: Thank you both. I passed a comfortable night.

Narrator: Since "Mr. Johnson" had one arm in a sling, William cut his master's food and then went out.

Captain 1: You have a very attentive slave, sir, but you had better watch him like a hawk when you get North. He seems all very well here, but he may act quite differently there. I've known many a gentleman who have lost their slaves among them cutthroat abolitionists.

Narrator: Before "Mr. Johnson" could speak, a man sitting across the table joined the conversation.

Slave Buyer: Sound doctrine, Captain, very sound. I would not take a slave North under no consideration. If you do, he's as good as gone. He'll run away the first chance he gets. Now, stranger, if you've a mind to sell that slave, I'm your man. Just mention your price, and if it isn't out of the way, I will pay for him right here and now in hard silver dollars. What do you say, stranger?

Ellen: I thank you for your offer, but I don't wish to sell, sir. I cannot get on well without him.

Slave Buyer: You will have to get on without him if you take him up North. I can tell you as a friend, he'll leave you the minute he crosses Mason and Dixon's line.

Ellen: I think not, sir. I have great confidence in William's fidelity.

Slave Buyer: Fidelity! Fidevil! You use a word like "fidelity" for a slave! It always makes me mad to hear a man talking about fidelity in slaves. There ain't a one of 'em who wouldn't take off if he had half a chance!

Captain 1: Excuse me, gentlemen, we are approaching Charleston. I am sure you all will want to go out on deck.

Ellen: Thank you, Captain, but I fear the sea air is too much for my constitution to bear. If you'll excuse me, sir, I'd best retire to my cabin.

Narrator: Ellen walked slowly back to the cabin, shaking with anger. William was waiting by the door for her return.

William: I could hear that slave buyer a-shouting clear out on deck. What'd he say?

Ellen: He offered to buy you, William! Thank goodness we're pulling into port. It looks as if we've made it to Charleston, South Carolina.

William: Just look at that crowd on the wharf. That could mean trouble for us. It's possible someone in that crowd might recognize me. We'd better wait until things clear out 'fore leaving the ship.

Ellen: I pray our absence hasn't been discovered. If it has been, they may have telegraphed for someone to stop us on shore.

Narrator: William and Ellen waited until all the other passengers had gone ashore. When they saw that no one lingered on the wharf, they took a carriage from the steamer to a hotel that Ellen had heard about. While "Mr. Johnson" rested, William took his master's boots out on the back steps to polish them. While he was sitting there, one of the hotel slaves engaged him in conversation.

Pompey: Where you headed, brother?

William: Philadelphia.

Pompey: Philadelphia! I hear there're no slaves in Philadelphia.

William: I heard the same.

Pompey: I surely do wish I was going with you! How you getting there?

© Macmillan/McGraw-Hill

William:	We're taking the steamer from Charleston to Philadelphia.
Pompey:	That's what you think—that steamer don't run in the winter, brother. You know, a few weeks back, they found a runaway slave hiding on board. They whipped him good and sent him back to his master.
William:	Poor soul! Well, I guess my master will know another way to Philadelphia.
Pompey:	I hope when you get there, you stay!
William:	Thank you, brother. I best be going now.
Narrator:	When William returned to the room with the well-shined boots, he told Ellen what he had learned.

William:	We gotta change our plans, Ellen. It may be just as well for us. Since that runaway slave was found, I got a suspicion they're going to check all the slaves mighty carefully.
Ellen:	I heard a passenger describing another way—the Overland Mail Route. We'd have to take a steamer to Wilmington, North Carolina, and a train from there to Philadelphia.
William:	We're all right then! We should leave right after dinner.
Narrator:	Upon leaving the hotel, William and Ellen took a carriage to the Charleston Custom House office. There "Mr. Johnson" would buy the tickets through to their final destination, Philadelphia—but not without obstacles.
Ellen:	Two tickets to Philadelphia, please. One for me and one for my slave.
Ticket Agent:	Just a minute, sir. . . . Hey you, come over here!
William:	You talking to me, sir?
Ticket Agent:	Of course I'm talking to you! Do you belong to this gentleman?

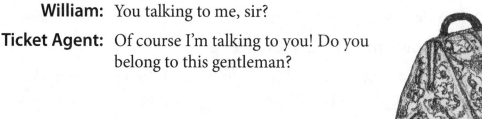

William: Yes, sir, I do.

Ticket Agent: That's all right then. Now, sir, I wish you to register your name here and also the name of your slave. You'll also have to pay a dollar duty on him.

Ellen: Here is the dollar, sir. But, as you can see, I cannot write because of my bandaged arm. Would you kindly register the names for me?

Ticket Agent: Regulations forbid me from doing that, sir! Either you register the names yourself or you'll not pass through my station.

Narrator: The man spoke so harshly that he attracted the attention of other passengers in the Custom House. It was a tense moment. Ellen found herself scarcely breathing. Just then, a passenger who had sat at breakfast with "Mr. Johnson" stepped forward. He patted "Mr. Johnson" on the shoulder and then turned to the ticket agent.

Passenger: See here, sir! Mr. Johnson is well known to me, and I will vouch for him. Anyone can see that he is un-well. There is no reason to treat him so unkindly.

Ticket Agent: I am simply following the rules, sir.

Captain 2: What is all this commotion about? I'm the captain of the steamer bound for Wilmington. We're about to leave, and these passengers must board. I will register the gentleman's name and assume the responsibility upon myself. Your full name, sir?

Ellen: William Johnson.

Captain 2: William Johnson and slave. There, it's done. Everything is in order now, Mr. Johnson.

Ellen: Thank you, Captain. You have my deepest gratitude, sir.

Captain 2: I'm sure the ticket agent intended no disrespect, Mr. Johnson. They have to be very vigilant in Charleston; otherwise, those blamed abolitionists might make off with any number of slaves.

Ellen: I am sure you are right, Captain. I am sure you are right.

Narrator: "Mr. Johnson" trembled at their narrow escape. How close they had come to being sent back! He could only imagine what other troubles might lie ahead.

Saturday, December 23, 1848
From Wilmington, North Carolina to Washington, D.C.

Narrator: William and Ellen reached Wilmington on the third morning of their journey. There they boarded a train that took them to Richmond and then on to Fredericksburg, Virginia. Outside Fredericksburg, they boarded a steamer bound for Washington, D.C. During the trip, "Mr. Johnson" met many white people whose kindness posed great danger. One man presented him with his business card. "Mr. Johnson" quickly put it in a pocket for he couldn't risk holding it upside down while pretending to read it! Two young ladies offered their shawls to make a pillow for the ailing gentleman. Evidently, the disguise was convincing. However, "Mr. Johnson" could never let down his guard. There was no way to know when danger might strike—or in what form.

Woman: Oh, my goodness, there goes my slave Ned. That's him, over there!

Ellen: Madam, I fear you are mistaken. That's my slave William!

Narrator: The woman paid no attention to "Mr. Johnson's" protests.

Woman: You, Ned, come here to me, you runaway!

Ellen: I assure you, madam, that you are mistaken!

Narrator: "Mr. Johnson's" blood ran cold. What would he do if the woman continued to insist that William was her Ned? Would he be asked to produce ownership papers?

Woman: Come closer, Ned. I know it's you, you rascal!

William: Excuse me, missus. I'm William.

Narrator: The woman looked closely at William and then turned to "Mr. Johnson."

Woman: Oh, I do beg your pardon, sir. I was so sure he was my Ned! But indeed you were right. I was mistaken.

Narrator: "Mr. Johnson" breathed a sigh of relief. Their luck had held once again. If only it would last a little longer.

Sunday, December 24, 1848
From Washington, D.C. to Baltimore, Maryland

Narrator: In Washington, William and Ellen hurried off to catch the train for Baltimore. They arrived in Baltimore on the evening of December 24. They had reached the most perilous stop on their long journey.

Ellen: Baltimore frightens me more than I can say, William. I should be happy that it's the last southern port we have to travel through. But I am more anxious than ever.

William: We got good reason for being fearful. The guards are everywhere on the lookout to keep slaves from crossing into Pennsylvania where they'd be free. But I can't believe we'll fail—not when we're so near our goal!

Narrator: William helped his master into the train. Then he made his way to the car in the back. Suddenly, he felt someone tapping his shoulder.

Conductor 2: Where are you going?

William: To Philadelphia, sir.

Conductor 2: What are you going there for?

William: I'm traveling with my master, sir. He's in a carriage up front, sir.

Conductor 2: Well, I calculate you had better get him out, and be mighty quick about it because the train will soon be starting. It's against railroad rules to let any man take a slave past here, unless he can satisfy them in the office that he has a right to take him along.

A Thousand Miles to Freedom 169

Narrator: William ran back to the carriage where he had left Ellen. Fortunately, "Mr. Johnson" was sitting quite alone.

William: How're you feeling, master?

Ellen: Much better, thank you. I'm glad we're getting on so nicely.

William: I'm afraid we're not getting on quite so well as we'd hoped.

Ellen: What do you mean? Is something the matter?

William: Mr. Johnson, sir, we gotta go into the station and prove I'm your slave.

Ellen: [whispering] Prove that you're my slave? But I have no proof! Oh, William, we've come so far! Is it possible that we're doomed after all to hopeless bondage?

William: [whispering] Ellen, now's the time we gotta call up our faith and courage. We'd best go in . . . and quickly.

Narrator: The two terror-stricken fugitives entered the station office. They both knew that their very existence was at stake; with this encounter, they would sink or swim. The office was crowded with travelers full of Christmas cheer. William and Ellen made their way to the station master's window. He eyed them suspiciously, but somehow Ellen managed to keep her head up and her voice firm.

Ellen: Do you wish to see me, sir?

Station Master: Yes. I hear you're traveling with a slave. It's against railroad rules, sir, to allow any person to take a slave out of Baltimore into Philadelphia, unless he can satisfy us that he has a right to take him along.

Ellen: Why is that?

Station Master: Because, sir, if we should allow any gentleman to take a slave past here into Philadelphia, and should that

gentleman not be the slave's owner, and should the proper master come and prove that his slave escaped on our railroad—then we would have to pay what the slave was worth. That's why!

Ellen: I understand, sir, but . . .

Station Master: Now, do you, or do you not, have proof that this is your slave?

Ellen: I do, sir, but I do not have it with me.

Narrator: Their conversation had attracted the attention of the other passengers, who seemed to sympathize with "Mr. Johnson" because he looked so ill. Seeing their reaction, the station master became more polite.

Station Master: Do you have some acquaintance in Baltimore who could assure us that this slave is your property?

Ellen: Alas no, sir, I do not. I bought tickets in Charleston to pass us through to Philadelphia, and therefore you have no right to detain us here in Baltimore.

Station Master: Well, sir, right or not, I shan't let you go through without proof that this is your slave!

Narrator: For a few minutes, there was total silence in the office. Ellen and William looked at each other. Neither dared speak a word for fear of making some blunder that would give them away. They knew that the railroad officers had the power to throw them into prison. Then they would be taken back to punishment and a life of slavery. They felt as though they were suspended over a pit by the thinnest of threads. Then suddenly, a large man pushed to the front of the crowd and approached the station master's window.

Onlooker: Where's your Christmas spirit, station master? Can't you see that this poor gentleman is sick? Have a heart. Let him go on to Philadelphia.

Station Master: That's easy for you to say, sir. It's not you who's taking the responsibility.

Narrator: Just then the bell rang for the train to leave. It came with the sudden shock of an earthquake. The office door opened; the conductor of the train stepped in. Every eye was fixed intently on the drama at the station master's window.

Station Master: Conductor, did these two come with you on the train from Washington?

Conductor 2: They surely did, sir! Going up to Philadelphia to see a special doctor, I understand. All right, everyone, we're ready to pull out.

Narrator: "Mr. Johnson" appealed to the station master again.

Ellen: Please allow me to board that train, sir. I am feeling faint and very weak.

Station Master: I really don't know what to do . . . . Oh-h-h, I calculate it's all right. Clerk, inform the conductor to let this gentleman and his slave pass. As he is not well, it's a pity to stop him here. We will let him go.

Ellen: Thank you, sir. Thank you! And a very Merry Christmas to you and your family.

Monday, December 25, 1848
From Baltimore, Maryland to Philadelphia, Pennsylvania

Narrator: William and Ellen boarded the train seconds before it pulled out of the station. Ellen collapsed into her seat. The train traveled on into the night, carrying them closer and closer to their final destination. Early on Christmas morning, the train pulled into the Philadelphia station. Before it even stopped, William leaped onto the platform and ran to get Ellen.

Ellen: We are safe, William! Safe and free!

William: Glory be, Ellen! We have been granted freedom for Christmas!

Narrator: The abolitionist William Lloyd Garrison recounted the Craft's harrowing escape in his newspaper, *The Liberator*. In 1850, two years after their flight to freedom, Ellen and William Craft moved to England for fear that if they stayed in the United States, they might be forced to return to their former masters under the provisions of the soon-to-be-enacted Fugitive Slave Act. With the assistance of a friend, William wrote a book titled *Running a Thousand Miles for Freedom*, which recounted the true story of their daring escape. The Crafts and their two children lived in England for eighteen years. They returned to the United States after the Civil War and bought a former plantation near Savannah, Georgia. There they established a school for black children and adults.

The Golden Door
by Myka-Lynne Sokoloff

CAST:

Characters from 1941:
Julia Conte
Maria Conte
Angelo Conte

Characters from 1906:
Giancarlo Conte
Young Angelo
Papa Minetti
Young Maria
Mama Minetti
Francesca Romano

Characters from 1906:
Sophia Balducci
Giuseppe Balducci
Paolo Romano
Gina Romano
Antonia Mancini
Salvatore Amato
Official
Lena Bonelli
Inspector
Fiorello La Guardia
Franco Bonforte

Julia: Mmmm! Grandma, the tomato sauce smells great!

Maria: Give it a stir, Julia, so it won't burn. My hands are covered with flour from the tortellini dough.

Julia: Sure, Grandma. Is there anything else I can do to help? Getting Thanksgiving dinner ready is a lot of work.

Maria: It is a lot of work, but having you here will help it go faster. Why don't you set the table? Use my good lace cloth; it's wrapped up in tissue paper in the second drawer of the sideboard.

Julia: Grandma, this cloth is beautiful! Is it old?

Maria: Old? I should say so! My oldest sister made that cloth for me as a wedding present when I married your grandpa thirty-five years ago. It was one of the few things I brought with me from Italy when we came to America.

Julia: Why didn't you bring everything you owned?

Maria: As a matter of fact, we did bring almost everything we owned—which wasn't much in those days, but even so it was almost more than we could carry! There were no porters in steerage, you know.

Julia: Steerage? What's steerage, Grandma?

Maria: What's steerage? Well, Julia, that's a long story.

Julia: Good, I love long stories, Grandma. Besides, it'll help to make up for the fact that I couldn't go to the parade with everyone else because of this stupid cold.

Maria: Very well, if you really want a lesson in family history, take a good look at the photo hanging above the sideboard.

Julia: You mean the picture with you and Grandpa in the middle?

Maria: Yes, it was taken in 1906 when your grandpa and I were first married. A traveling photographer came to the town where Grandpa and I grew up outside of Naples.

Julia: Grandpa looks so young!

Maria: He was young—just twenty years old! Standing beside him is his older brother, Giancarlo Conte.

Julia: Uncle Giancarlo. . . . Isn't that who my brother Johnny was named after?

Maria: Yes, and he was the one who first put the idea of immigrating to America into Grandpa's head!

SOUND EFFECT: [clock ticking]

Giancarlo: I tell you, Angelo, it's getting harder to make a living every year. Now I can see it was a mistake to cut down so many olive and fruit trees to plant more grapevines. This grape disease is killing off our whole vineyard.

Young Angelo: It's true, Giancarlo, and to make things worse, the wine we made from last year's grapes isn't selling.

Papa Minetti: Buon giorno, Giancarlo and Angelo. How's my new son-in-law?

Young Angelo: Buon giorno, Papa Minetti. I was just telling Giancarlo that I can't understand why last year's wine isn't selling.

Papa Minetti: We're not the only ones who've been affected. I heard from my cousin in Bologna that everyone in Italy is having the same problem.

Young Angelo: Did your cousin say why?

Papa Minetti: Well, he said that a few years ago, the vineyards in France were hit with the same disease that's killing our vines now. When that happened, the French had no choice but to buy Italian wine. But now their vines are healthy again, and there's no longer a shortage of French wine. So they aren't buying Italian wine anymore.

© Macmillan/McGraw-Hill

Young Angelo: Wine isn't the only thing that isn't selling. Our fruit is rotting by the bushel.

Giancarlo: That's true enough! I read in a newspaper that the Americans have stopped buying from us because they've planted their own orange and lemon orchards. The Americans are also growing more grapes, apricots, and walnuts than we are!

Papa Minetti: Yes, and they have fast trains to take that fruit to places like New York City, where we used to sell our products. Our markets are disappearing.

Young Angelo: Just trying to get something to grow in this worn-out soil is hard enough. If it's not a disease killing the grapes, there's a drought to deal with.

Giancarlo: I've heard they don't have droughts in America like we have here.

Papa Minetti: A drought is a bad thing, but when the rains come, that means more mosquitoes, which makes the malaria worse!

Giancarlo: I've heard they don't have mosquitoes or malaria in America, either!

Julia: Malaria! Grandma, didn't that scare you?

Maria: Of course it did! We were all frightened by the mere thought of malaria, but there was something that scared me even more.

SOUND EFFECT: [rumbling; dishes rattling]

Giancarlo: Another earthquake!

The Golden Door 177

Young Angelo: It's just a little tremor. I usually sleep right through them, but Maria doesn't. Ever since the earthquake in Calabria killed all those people last year, she jumps whenever a cart rumbles by the house. Every time the ground shakes, she's sure Mount Vesuvius is going to erupt again. She thinks we'll all be buried in ashes, just like Pompeii.

Giancarlo: You know, Angelo, if I didn't have a wife, six children, and Mama and Papa living under my roof, I'd think about leaving.

Young Angelo: Leaving! Where would you go?

Giancarlo: Why, to America, the land of opportunity!

Maria: Shortly after that, our neighbor Luigi got a letter from his brother Franco, who had immigrated to America. Franco said there were plenty of jobs in America for people who were willing to work hard.

SOUND EFFECT: [clock ticking]

Young Maria: What is it, Angelo? You look so worried.

Young Angelo: Can you read my face so clearly? Well, since you asked, I'll tell you. I don't know what to do, Maria. Most of our vineyard has been wiped out; this farm can't support my parents, my brother's family, and the two of us.

Young Maria: Perhaps you could find work up north.

Young Angelo: There are no jobs up north. . . . I've asked. When we got married, I promised your parents that I would provide a good life for you. I meant that. When we have a family, I don't want to worry about how we're going to feed our children.

Young Maria: What can we do, Angelo?

Young Angelo: Maria, what would you say if I told you I wanted us to go to America? You've heard Luigi tell about his brother's letters. If we work hard, we could have a future there. If we stay in Italy, we will always be poor.

Young Maria: Ai, Angelo, think what we'd be giving up if we did leave—your parents and mine, all of our relatives and friends! I don't know if I could bear that.

Young Angelo: I know it would be hard to leave everyone behind, but I think it's our only chance for a better life. What do you say, Maria?

Young Maria: I think you're right, Angelo; there is no future here. Maybe if we worked hard and saved our earnings, we could send passage money for our families to join us in America in a few years.

Young Angelo: Of course we could! That's what Luigi's brother is doing.

Young Maria: Then we'll do it. We'll go to America.

Julia: After you made the decision, did you just pack up and move to America, Grandma?

Maria: No, Julia, it was a little more complicated than that. Once we'd made our decision, we talked to everyone who knew anyone who'd already immigrated to America. We wrote to Luigi's brother, who agreed to help us find a home and a job in New York. . . . Here's the silverware, Julia. You finish setting the table while I baste the turkey. . . . Now, let's see, where was I? Oh, yes. We didn't have quite enough money, so we had to borrow from our families to pay for the steamer tickets. We didn't own many things, so we didn't have to worry too much about what to pack. Finally, the day came when our ship was scheduled to sail.

SOUND EFFECT: [boat whistle]

Giancarlo: Ciao, Maria. Ciao, Angelo!

Papa Minetti: We'll miss you, cara mia. Send us a letter as soon as you get to America.

Mama Minetti: Maria, take these sausages and cheese that Papa made. You never know what they'll feed you on the boat. I'll miss you so and I'll think of you every day.

Young Maria: Oh, Mama, Papa! I'll miss you, too—more than I can say. I'll write to you as soon as we find a place to live.

Papa Minetti: You're a brave girl, Maria. Have a safe voyage.

Mama Minetti: Arrivederci! Have a good trip, my daughter!

Young Angelo: Come, Maria, let's find our berths and stow our luggage. The steward said that steerage is down these steps.

Young Maria: It's so dark. I can hardly see where I'm going.

Young Angelo: I think this is the right place.

Young Maria: Is this where we're to sleep? There's one bunk on top of another on top of another! Angelo, it's so dark and the smells are so awful! I hope I don't get sick!

Francesca: Excuse me, signora, but you can't put that basket there. Someone is bound to trip over it.

Young Maria: Where am I to put it?

Francesca: I'm not sure. I've been searching for a cupboard or locker to put things in, but I don't think there are any in steerage. Maybe we're supposed to keep all our belongings on our bunks!

Young Maria: On our bunks? There won't be enough room to turn over!

Julia: Grandma, what was steerage? You never told me.

Maria: Steerage was the cheapest way to travel across the Atlantic Ocean in those days. Passengers with steerage tickets rode in the large compartments below the decks and near the steering mechanism. There was almost no fresh air to speak of, and we heard the pounding noise of the engines day and night. Since the tickets were inexpensive, the steamship companies packed people in as tight as could be. There were over one thousand steerage passengers on the ship that your grandpa and I took and larger steamships carried even more!

Julia: It sounds awful!

Maria: Actually, Grandpa and I were lucky. Because we were traveling on an Italian ship, there were lots of Italians on board to talk with. On a trip like that, there wasn't much to do except talk.

Julia: How long did the voyage take?

Maria: The trip from Naples to New York took two weeks. Here, Julia, drop the tortellini into the broth while I make the turkey gravy. Then taste it and tell me if it needs more seasoning.

Julia: Mmmm, perfect! This tortellini soup tastes wonderful. I'll bet you didn't eat like this on the ship.

Maria: Oh, the stories I could tell you about the food on that ship! People brought their own food from home and cooked it right there in that cramped room with those berths stacked to the ceiling. The smell of cabbage and fish was more than some people could bear.

SOUND EFFECT: [banging of pots and spoons]

Sophia: I don't feel very well.

Young Maria: Can't we get some air in here? Won't someone please try to get one of those windows open?

Giuseppe: Every time my wife feels sick, I open a window. But as soon as I do, someone from the ship's crew closes it.

Young Angelo: Why is that, Signore Balducci?

Giuseppe: Down here in steerage, we're so close to the level of the water that they're afraid the waves will rush in and drown us!

Sophia: Ohhh, can't somebody do something?

Young Maria: Here, I'll go to the washroom to wet a cloth to put on your forehead. Maybe that will make you feel better, Signora Balducci.

Francesca: Ah, Signora Conte, I hope you're not in a hurry. I've been waiting in this line for over an hour just to get to the sink.

Paolo: Mama, how come there's only one washroom for this whole compartment?

Gina: Si, Mama, and why does the tap have only cold saltwater?

Francesca: Ah, children, it would be different if we were first- or second-class passengers, but we couldn't have afforded the cost of those tickets in a million years! In steerage, we should count ourselves lucky to have this one tap to wash our pots, our laundry, and ourselves.

Paolo: Si, and if anyone gets seasick . . .

Francesca: Paolo, that's enough.

Young Maria: He's right, Signora Romano, we're packed in steerage like cattle! If only we didn't have to cook and eat in here, too. The smell is just too much for poor Signora Balducci. Our only hope is for good weather so that we can go up on deck and breathe!

Julia: Grandma! What a miserable way to travel! The whole trip must have been a nightmare!

Maria: There was no question about it, traveling across the Atlantic in steerage was an ordeal. Fortunately, we had a smooth crossing. Whenever we could, we went up on deck to dance and talk.

SOUND EFFECT: [violin or accordion music playing a tarantella]

Francesca: I hope you're feeling better now, Signora Balducci.

Sophia: Yes, I am, thank you. Even if it is a little chilly, at least the air is better up here on deck than below.

Francesca: That's certainly true. And as long as it's such a pleasant day, let's talk of pleasant things and forget about steerage for awhile. Where are you and your family going when you get to America, Signora Balducci?

Sophia: We're planning to take a train to a town called Chicago, where my brother and his family live. We'll stay with them until my husband finds work and we find a place to live. What about you, Signorina Mancini?

Antonia: I'm engaged to be married when I get to New York. The man I'm to wed came from a small village near mine back in Italy, but we've never met before.

Young Maria: How will you know him when we arrive?

Antonia: My papa sent him my photograph so he can recognize me, but I've no idea what he looks like. What if he didn't send me his photograph because he's pockmarked or has no teeth? I never dared tell my parents this, but I'm really very nervous about marrying someone I've never even seen before.

Francesca: Don't worry, signorina. I barely knew my husband when I married him. Now we have three children, and I can't wait to see him again. It's been two years since he went to America.

Gina: Papa has a job in a factory in Boston, but he's coming to New York to meet us.

Paolo: I've grown so much, Papa probably won't even recognize me!

Francesca: Don't worry, Paolo, he'll recognize you. You look just like him! Now, let's hear your plans, Signora Conte.

Young Maria: We're being met by a neighbor's brother who lives on Mulberry Street in New York City. He's a bricklayer, and he's promised to help my husband find a job. Then, once we get settled, I'll work, too, and at night, Angelo and I will go to school to learn English!

Julia: It must have been exciting to talk about all your plans and dreams.

Maria: Oh, yes, it was. We were all so young and so full of hope. For all of us, America was a vivid dream; it seemed to offer the promise of a bright future. But there were other discussions before we reached New York—discussions that were not as cheerful.

SOUND EFFECT: [wind; rain; water slapping against the ship]

Salvatore: When we get to America, our first stop will be Ellis Island. Now, before they'll give you a landing card, you have to pass an inspection. According to my cousin, you have to be very careful about what you tell the inspectors. They ask you lots of questions— bang, bang, bang—without giving you any time at all to think! And heaven help you if you give a wrong answer!

Giuseppe: And you'd better have enough money to show them, too. If they think you might not be able to support yourself, forget it! They'll put you on the next boat back to Italy!

Salvatore: My cousin says they try to trick you. If you say you've got a job, it's no good. If you say you don't know what you're gonna do, it's no good. You really have to be careful what you say.

Young Angelo: Well, what is the best way to answer?

Salvatore: Tell them you have a trade, you're strong, and you're willing to work hard. That's the best thing.

Sophia: My brother wrote telling me what to expect. He said they'll check you all over from head to foot. They'll look at your hands, they'll listen to you breathe, then they'll watch you walk. When they're all done with that, he said they'll poke you in the eye with a buttonhook!

Gina: Mama! I don't want to get poked in the eye with a hook!

Francesca: Don't worry, cara mia, they don't really poke you in the eye, they just look under your eyelid.

Young Maria: Why would they want to do that?

Sophia: They're looking for an eye disease that causes blindness. Last year, a woman from my village went over, and they discovered she had this disease. They sent her right back home on the next boat! They wouldn't even let her say good-bye to the rest of her family!

Young Maria: Oh, Angelo, how dreadful!

Young Angelo: Yes, it is, but there's nothing wrong with our eyes. I'm sure we'll be all right.

Julia: Grandma, you must have been so frightened. I can't imagine what it must have been like—going off to a strange land and hearing all those scary stories on the ship!

Maria: Yes, Julia, after fourteen days of that kind of talk, all of us were terrified about what lay ahead on the Island of Tears. That's what Ellis Island was sometimes called. Some of the stories told aboard the ship were exaggerated, but many of them were true.

Julia:	Tell me what happened when you finally got to New York, Grandma.
Maria:	Well, before we left Italy, we believed that America was the land of the free. But when we reached its gates, we learned that you were free only if you'd purchased a first- or second-class steamship ticket.
SOUND EFFECT:	[boat whistle]
Official:	Attention, Attenzione, Achtung! Passengers should prepare to disembark. All passengers must carry their own papers. Steerage passengers should carry their belongings to the gangplank. Make sure the number cards you were given are securely pinned to your chest.
Young Angelo:	Say, Salvatore, do you understand what's going on? What are these numbers for?
Salvatore:	According to what my brother told me, one is our ship number and the other is a code for the passenger lists. That way, the inspectors can ask us questions and check to see that our answers match those we gave to the ticket agents back in Naples.
Young Maria:	Look, the first-class passengers are leaving already. Why is that?
Francesca:	Their first-class tickets permit them to leave the ship without an examination.
Salvatore:	That's right. The inspectors assume that those who can afford first-class tickets will be able to support themselves in America.
Young Angelo:	What about the second-class passengers? What happens to them?
Salvatore:	Oh, they get examined on the ship, and then they're free to go. Once the first- and second-class passengers have gone ashore, they'll take the rest of us over to Ellis Island on a ferry.

© Macmillan/McGraw-Hill

Official: All second-class passengers who have been examined may go ashore. Steerage passengers, collect your belongings and line up to board the ferry.

Julia: Grandma, they really discriminated against steerage passengers! Why didn't they treat everyone the same?

Maria: That's a good question, Julia. You have to keep in mind that most of the people who traveled steerage class in those days were very poor. The authorities were afraid that those who were physically or mentally ill, or without any resources at all, wouldn't be able to take care of themselves.

Julia: I guess there were a lot of people coming into this country then.

Maria: There certainly were. Remember, on our ship alone, there were over a thousand of us in steerage! The United States government wanted to avoid the expense of caring for immigrants who couldn't take care of themselves, so we had to endure those terrifying inspections.

Julia: Well, it doesn't seem fair to me. I thought everyone was supposed to be welcome. That's why the Statue of Liberty is in the harbor. Oh, Grandma, tell me about the first time you saw the Statue of Liberty.

Maria: Ai! I'll never forget the first time I saw her. It was a rainy day when our ship steamed into New York harbor, and we could see very little because of the fog. Despite the rain, all of us were on deck, straining to catch a glimpse of land and Lady Liberty. For a long time, there was nothing but the fog and the sound of water against the hull. Then suddenly, she seemed to rise up out of the mist, holding her torch like a beacon to us.

Julia: It sounds like something from a wonderful dream.

Maria: It was like a dream. Some people cheered; others fell to their knees and wept. You know the poem that Emma Lazarus wrote about her? The part that goes . . .

Give me your tired, your poor,
Your huddled masses yearning to breathe free,
The wretched refuse of your teeming shore.

Julia: Send these, the homeless, tempest-tost, to me. I lift my lamp beside the golden door!

Maria: Yes, that's it. The poem described us perfectly. After two weeks in that dreadful steerage compartment, we were wretched, homeless, and tempest-tost, believe me. But even so, we were overjoyed when we first caught sight of Lady Liberty. She reminded us of the promise of America. But we still had to get through the Island of Tears.

SOUND EFFECT: [foghorn; rain]

Young Angelo: Are you cold, Maria?

Young Maria: Yes, I'm soaked to the skin, and that wind is so cold. If only we didn't have to stand here in the rain! It's not so bad for us, but I worry about the children and the old people. They shouldn't be out in weather like this.

Young Angelo: I wish I knew what was happening. We've been waiting on this ferry with no food or water for hours.

Giuseppe: There are so many people coming to America that they can't examine us fast enough. And they won't let us off this ferry until there's room for us on the island.

Young Angelo: Do you know just how many immigrants we're talking about?

Paolo: My father wrote that over 12,000 people went through Ellis Island in just one day a few months ago!

Salvatore: Ah, we're beginning to move at last. Listen, my advice to you is to keep all your belongings with you when you get off. My cousin said that his baggage was stolen from the luggage area while he went through the inspections. If they don't steal your bags outright, they may charge you several months' wages just to get them back!

Young Angelo: Did you hear that, Maria? I think you'd better carry the basket and the bundle, and I'll manage the trunk. We'll keep everything with us—just to be safe.

Young Maria: I'll wrap the remaining sausages and cheese in my shawl; they don't fit in the basket.

Julia: Grandma, what were you and Grandpa carrying in your luggage?

Maria: Well, if I remember correctly, I had the tablecloth my sister made for me, this candelabra, which was my mother's. . . . You should put it in the center of the table. That's a good girl. Let's see . . . we also had a jug of olive oil from my father's olives, a couple of photographs, two comforters, and feather pillows.

Julia: What about extra clothes?

Maria: Each of us had one change of clothing, and besides that, we still had a bit of food from the boat. That was it. I know it doesn't sound like much, but it all got very heavy before the end of that long day!

Julia: What happened when you finally got to Ellis Island?

Maria: First, we lined up under a long canopy at the entrance to the main building. Then, ever so slowly, we moved toward the heavy doors that opened into this huge room called the Great Hall. As soon as we entered, I dropped my bundles and covered up both ears! The sound was unbelievable—thousands of people laughing and crying, talking, shouting, and even screaming, all at the same time. It was so loud you cannot imagine it! Directly ahead of us was a staircase that rose more than fifty feet up to the second floor.

The Golden Door **189**

SOUND EFFECT: [roar of many voices]

Young Angelo: Why is it taking so long just to "climb the stairs to the second floor?"

Salvatore: See those inspectors standing at the top of the stairs? Well, my cousin told me that they stand there watching to see who has problems. If they see you have trouble breathing or if you limp, they'll put a chalk mark on your coat.

Young Angelo: A chalk mark? Whatever for?

Salvatore: They have different letter codes to show who needs to be looked at more carefully by the doctors. Some of the people who get chalk marks will be sent back.

Young Maria: Did you see that woman in the long, silk coat? The inspector chalked an H on her coat. She just turned her coat inside out!

Giuseppe: Clever woman! That way, the next inspector won't see the chalk mark, and she won't be sent home.

Young Angelo: Maria, look at that man. They put a different mark on his back. Watch him brush against the wall. I think they're going to miss the mark. It's all smudged now. What a bold fellow he is!

Julia: Did they put any chalk marks on you or Grandpa?

Maria: No, child, both of us were young and healthy. When we got to the top of the stairs, we passed the medical inspectors in a matter of seconds. Then we saw that the second floor was divided by iron bars into passageways to keep us in line. We moved slowly up and down each row. At the end of the last row was the dreaded eye inspection! A medical officer placed a buttonhook under my upper eyelid. Then he folded my eyelid over so that he could get a good look at my eyeball to check for signs of trachoma. Although the examination was painful, it was over in a minute, and the doctor waved me on. I was so relieved.

Julia: Then were you free to leave?

Maria: Oh, no! We had only passed the physical part of the inspection. There we were in a huge room with a high ceiling that magnified every sound even more. People were speaking at least a dozen different languages, children were crying, there was the shuffling of thousands of feet—I tell you, the noise from the engines in steerage was nothing compared to the noise in that room!

Julia: Could you at least sit down and rest?

Maria: Yes, we were told to sit on some wooden benches with other passengers from our ship. As the bench in front emptied, we had to pick up our belongings and move up. At that point, I was so tired I think I fell asleep holding onto my basket and bundle, with my papers clutched between my teeth.

SOUND EFFECT: [roar of many voices]

Young Angelo: Maria, Maria, wake up. We have to move up to the front bench. Here's something to eat. All the vendor had left was prune sandwiches.

Young Maria: At least it's a change from the boiled potatoes, sausage, and cheese we've been eating for the last two weeks.

Young Angelo: I think they're almost ready for us at the interrogation desk. Try to eat something before they call our names.

Lena: Buon giorno. I see your number tags are different from mine. You must have come on another ship. Where are you from?

Young Maria: We're from Capua, near Naples, in Italy.

Lena: So, you went through the inspection all right?

Young Maria: Yes, so far.

Lena: You see that family over there? Such a pity. They took the little girl away to see if she has tuberculosis. The whole family must sleep here in the dormitory until the doctors decide what to do with the child. If she is consumptive, they'll send her back, that's for certain.

Young Maria: And you, are you well? You look so very tired.

Lena: I stayed here all night waiting for my husband to come. He left Italy two years ago. They won't release me until he, or another man in my family, comes to get me.

Young Maria: Angelo! I feel so sorry for these people.

Young Angelo: I know how you feel. . . . Come, Maria, that inspector is pointing at us. It's our turn to go.

Inspector: You! You're next. Do you speak English?

Young Angelo: Signore?

Inspector: Parla Italiano?

Young Angelo: Si.

Inspector: Italian interpreter—over here please!

La Guardia: Your names, please.

Young Angelo: Angelo and Maria Conte.

La Guardia: What boat did you come on, Signore Conte?

Young Angelo: Citta di Napoli.

La Guardia: Where were you born?

Young Angelo: Capua, in Italy.

La Guardia: Who paid for your passage?

Young Angelo: My wife and I saved our money.

La Guardia: How much money did you bring with you?

Young Angelo: Many lire.

La Guardia: Let me see it, please.

Young Angelo: But it's all I have left.

La Guardia: Don't worry, Signore Conte. We don't keep it. We just need to know that you've enough money to live on until you find a job. Signore, you have almost thirty-eight dollars here. It's not quite the twenty-five dollars apiece that you're supposed to have, but you look honest and hardworking to me.

Julia: Grandma, did he mark you with chalk since you didn't have enough money?

Maria: No, bambina, he was a good man. He told us that his own parents were emigrants from Italy, like us. Since he spoke seven languages, he was in great demand as an interpreter. He told us he worked at Ellis Island to pay his way through law school.

SOUND EFFECT: [roar of many voices; commotion]

Inspector: Interpreter, you speak Hungarian don't you? You're needed over there. I'll ask the last of these questions.

La Guardia: Excuse me, Signore Conte, I'm needed elsewhere. There are only a few simple questions left that the immigration inspector should be able to ask you.

Inspector: Who is meeting you here?

Young Angelo: Signore?

Inspector: WHO MEET YOU HERE?

Young Angelo: Oh. My friend brother.

Inspector: What is your brother's name?

Young Angelo: Giancarlo Conte.

Inspector: Do you have a job?

Young Angelo: No, no job, yet. Work hard.

Inspector: Well, you look strong enough. I guess you'll do fine. Now, how much is two plus two?

Young Angelo: Signore?

Inspector: TWO PLUS TWO. Oh, never mind. Interpreter, I need you back over here.

La Guardia: What's left to ask? Let's see. . . . How much is two plus two?

Young Angelo: Are you joking?

La Guardia: No, signore, I'm sorry, but I have to ask.

Young Angelo: Four.

La Guardia: Have you ever been in jail?

Young Angelo: No!

La Guardia: All right, that's all the questions you need to answer. Please go to that bench over there and wait until your names are called.

Julia: So you and Grandpa came through the interrogation with no problem?

Maria: We'd gotten through the interrogation, all right, but we were not yet free to go. We still had to wait for Luigi's brother, who was to come to meet us. We were a little nervous about identifying him, because we had never met him before. All we had to go by was his photograph!

SOUND EFFECT: [roar of many voices]

Inspector: Signore and Signora Angelo Conte, step forward! All right, point out the man who is meeting you. Look over there through the fence.

Young Angelo: There he is—the man wearing the gray cap. He looks like the man in the photograph I have.

Inspector: You, in the gray cap—what's your name?

Bonforte: Franco Bonforte.

Inspector: Bonforte. Your name isn't Conte? How are you related to this man?

Bonforte: Me? I'm not related to him.

Inspector: You, Conte—come here! What do you mean telling me your brother was meeting you? This man isn't related to you. He doesn't even know you. How dare you try to sneak into this country under false pretenses! Did you think you could fool the American government? I'm of a mind to put you on the very next boat back to Naples.

Young Maria: Ai! Angelo! What's wrong? That man is so angry with you! What happened? I can't understand what he's saying.

Young Angelo: I can't understand him, either, Maria. But I know I haven't done anything wrong. At least, I don't think I have.

Young Maria: Look, there's that nice interpreter. Maybe he can help.

Young Angelo: Per favore, signore. Can you please help us?

La Guardia: Excuse me. Is there some sort of misunderstanding here?

Inspector: I'll say there is! See if you can figure it out. This fellow told me his brother Giancarlo Conte was meeting him. But the man he's pointed out insists that he's no relation. Find out what's going on.

La Guardia: Signore Conte, who did you say was meeting you here?

Young Angelo: I told the inspector that my friend's brother was to meet us. Then he asked me for the name of my brother. I thought it was just another question to see if my answers matched the ones I'd given when I was questioned in Italy. Anyway, my friend's brother is Franco Bonforte. See, I have his photograph right here.

La Guardia: He says his friend's brother is meeting them.

Inspector: Oh, I thought he said his brother.

La Guardia: Well, it certainly looks like the right man. What did you say your name was, sir?

Bonforte: Franco Bonforte. I'm supposed to meet Angelo Conte and his wife, Maria.

La Guardia: Here they are. Just a minor misunderstanding, but now it looks like everything is cleared up. Here are your landing cards, Signore and Signora Conte. You're free to go. Welcome to America, and may you have a long and prosperous life in your new country.

Young Maria: Grazie. Thank you so much for helping us!

La Guardia: It's just part of my job, signora. Good luck!

Young Angelo: Maria, look, it's Signora Romano and her children, and that must be her husband.

Young Maria: They look so happy! And she was right, Angelo, young Paolo looks just like his papa. Oh, and look over there, standing next to the priest. It's Signorina Mancini and a nice-looking young man. They must be getting married right here on Ellis Island! Let's go over and wish them well.

Julia: So then they let you into the country?

Maria: Yes, we went to the money changer to exchange our lire for American dollars. Then we took the ferry to Manhattan, and from the ferryboat dock, made the quick trip to Mulberry Street. We lived there in a tiny two-room apartment above a grocery store until your father was born. Then we moved here to Brooklyn. . . . Oh, my! Look at the clock. Everyone will be home from the parade soon, and we still have a few things to do to get ready.

© Macmillan/McGraw-Hill

Julia: Did you ever have any regrets about coming here, Grandma?

Maria: No, never, at least not after that day on Ellis Island. We were all so fearful of being sent home every step of the way that the stories were harsher than the reality. Actually, only two people in a hundred were turned away. For those few, it was indeed an Island of Tears. But, for your grandpa and me, as for most others, it was a golden door—like in the poem—a golden door to the land of opportunity.

SOUND EFFECT: [door bell]

Julia: I'll get it, Grandma. . . . Hi, everybody, dinner's almost ready! How was the parade, Grandpa?

Angelo: The balloons and floats were even better than last year, Julia. I'm just sorry that you had to miss it.

Julia: I was, too, until Grandma started telling me all about your trip to America. What an exciting story! The time just flew by.

Angelo: That's a funny coincidence. Something happened at the parade that reminded me of our trip to America, too. In fact, I can hardly wait to tell your grandmother.

Maria: Tell me what, Angelo? Did you enjoy the parade? Did you hear the mayor's speech?

Angelo: Yes, we did. But, Maria, I had the most unbelievable surprise. Do you remember that terrible mix-up with the inspector at Ellis Island when we were afraid we would be sent back on the next boat?

Maria: Of course I do! How could I forget that? Why do you ask?

Angelo: Well, Maria, do you also happen to recall that kind young interpreter who helped us out? The one who made sense of the whole misunderstanding and stamped our papers for us?

Maria: I'll never forget him. He was a good man.

Angelo: Well, I saw him again today—more than thirty years later!

Maria: Was he at the parade?

Angelo: Yes, indeed, and you'll never guess who he is! It wasn't until I saw the mayor today and heard him speak that I realized that the interpreter who helped us get into this country was none other than Fiorello La Guardia!

Julia: Fiorello La Guardia! Why, he's the mayor of New York City!

Maria: Ai! What a wonderful country this is! The child of immigrants can become the mayor of the largest city in the nation. Now everybody come to the table! We have so much to be thankful for!

JANE ADDAMS AND HULL HOUSE

by Navidad O'Neill, 1996

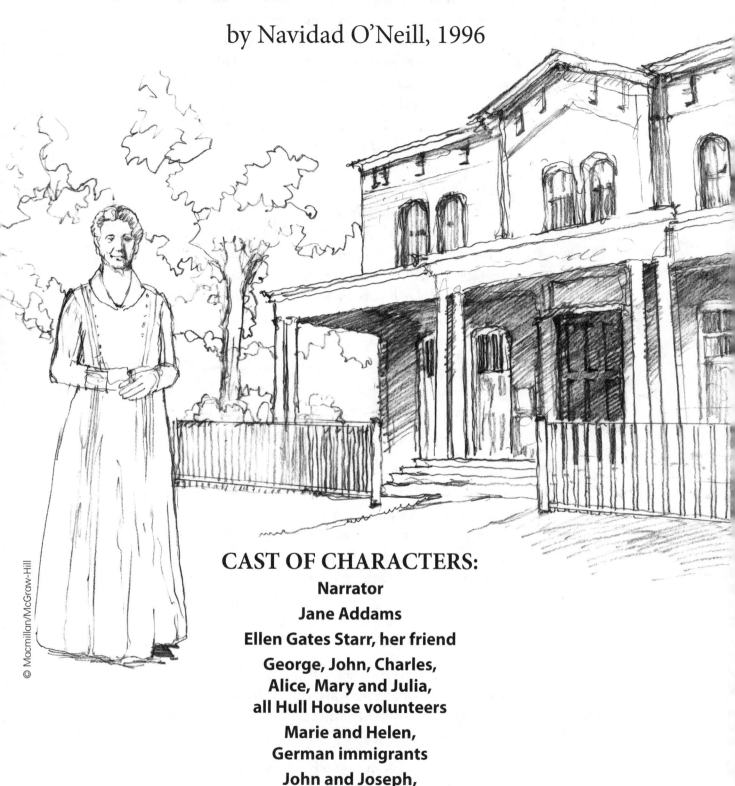

CAST OF CHARACTERS:

Narrator

Jane Addams

Ellen Gates Starr, her friend

**George, John, Charles,
Alice, Mary and Julia,
all Hull House volunteers**

**Marie and Helen,
German immigrants**

**John and Joseph,
Italian immigrants**

In the early 1900s many immigrants came to the United States to find a better way of life. Unfortunately, the way was not always easy for them. Many were poor and did not speak English. Others worked long hours in factories and mines for very little pay. Jane Addams decided that she had to do something for the poor. At first she decided to share her knowledge of art and literature, but soon she realized that they had more basic needs that had to be met. She and her friend, Ellen Starr, opened Hull House, the first settlement house in our country. Why do you think Jane Addams and her friend wished to help the poor?

Jane Addams should be alone at the beginning of the play. Either the playing area can be set with empty chairs or each character can bring in a chair when entering. The narrator serves the tea, either by miming it, or by bringing in new tea cups for each character. The effect should be of the play beginning with one person and then accumulating and expanding throughout until the end.

〜〜〜〜〜〜〜〜〜〜〜〜〜

Narrator: Jane Addams sits down to tea and ponders her future—and that of others.

Jane: In Chicago, there are people who sit in their large comfortable homes and drink tea. But in the slums of Chicago there are many people who live in small, crowded apartments. Sometimes 9 people live in one room. There is no time to sit down and rest because many of them work 16 hours a day. I wish I could do something to help them. But what? And how? What should I do with my life that would help change people's lives for the better?

Narrator: (A doorbell rings off-stage, or the narrator rings a bell to indicate each new arrival.) Jane is joined by Ellen Gates Starr, her friend from college, who sits down with her for tea.

Jane: I am sick of asking myself what I am and what I ought to be, Ellen.

Ellen: You haven't been happy since our return from England.

Jane: Ahhh. England. Remember Toynbee Hall, Ellen? Wasn't it inspiring? There in the middle of the London slums is a place where educated men and women share their knowledge and their lives with those around them. There they teach people how to read, how to paint, how to write, and how to sing. They help them get jobs and live full lives.

Ellen: Yes, I remember our visit there. The young men and women of Toynbee Hall live and work among the poor. They don't simply hand out food on holidays.

Jane: Do you think we could create a "Settlement" house like Toynbee Hall, here in Chicago where surely it is needed?

Ellen: Jane, I think you could create anything. You never think anything is too difficult, once you set your mind to it.

Jane: Would you help me?

Ellen: What do we do first?

Jane: Find a large table. And a large house in which to place it.

Narrator: (Doorbell rings) It is one month later. Jane and Ellen are joined by George, John, Charles, Alice, Mary, and Julia, who discuss how they can volunteer their time to make Hull House work.

Jane: Welcome, one and all, to Hull House. So do we all know our assignments for today?

George: I'm trying to locate more books for our library. We have the complete works of Shakespeare, but I think we could use more Greek classics and drama. We have many people from Greece in the neighborhood who would appreciate such literature.

Mary: I've purchased the paints and will set up the easels in the sunroom for the art classes that begin tonight.

John: The cribs for the child care room will be delivered this afternoon. I'll need help putting them together.

Ellen: I'll help you with that.

John: Great. There are 12 of them. There is a desperate need for a place where babies can be cared for while their parents are at work.

Julia: I'm going to find out how many children are actually working in factories 12 hours a day. I believe some are as young as five years old.

Jane: Do you want my help with that?

Julia: Not just yet. I'll let you know when it's time to present our findings to the American public. Then, when they know the facts, hopefully we can start to change this situation.

Charles: I'll see if I can get a doctor to volunteer to give the babies the shots they need.

Jane: Great. Try Dr. Alice Hamilton. She said she wanted to help.

Charles: Jane, what about the problem of garbage on the streets?

Ellen: It's not collected on a regular schedule and when the workers do collect it, they often dump it a block away. Last week a horse died in the middle of the street, and it's still there.

Julia: This is a serious problem. It's unhealthy for everyone who lives nearby.

Jane: I'll see what I can do. If I have to, I'll follow the garbage wagons all the way to the city dump to make sure the garbage is properly disposed of.

John: Would you really do that?

Jane: Why not? That's our job, to do anything it takes to make things better in our community.

Mary: Oh, and another thing. Jane, I think we need to buy more tables.

Narrator: (Doorbell rings again.) It is two weeks later. The neighborhood comes to Hull House for tea, and finds many reasons to stay.

Marie: I'm bringing my embroidered curtains. Miss Addams wants us to display our best work.

Helen: But Marie, what will you put on your windows in the meantime?

Marie: Plain, ordinary curtains. I want to save my best work for the Labor Museum, where all of the neighborhood can see it. What are you bringing, Helen?

Helen: You know the church I made from cookies and sweets?

Marie: With the steeple of cookies and the sugar-stained glass?

Helen: Yes. We will put that on display, on a high shelf where little hands won't be able to reach it and take a bite!

Marie: This Labor Museum is a good idea. Miss Addams said she noticed some of the young people thinking that the new ways people do things in the United States are better than what they call the old-fashioned ways of their parents.

Helen: We'll show them "old-fashioned"! We'll teach them to be proud of their culture and of what good things the "old folks" can make.

Marie: Miss Addams said there will be many guests at the opening of the Labor Museum. Even the newspaper reporters will be there.

Helen: We should tell Elsa to bring her needlepoint.

Marie: And Hubert should display his clocks.

Helen: Let's tell all of our neighbors.

(The narrator rings the doorbell. Joseph and John take tea at another table.)

John: Someone told me that Miss Addams got the idea for her Labor Museum from you. Is that true?

Joseph: I don't know if it's true, but I do know that she came to visit my wife and I one night and stood admiring the stairpost I had carved in our hallway.

John: The one with the angels?

Joseph: Yes, that's the one. She said, "This should be on display for the whole neighborhood to see." And then she asked me if I would bring something else I had carved.

John: My wife told me that Miss Addams wanted me to bring in one perfect tomato to show in this museum of our labors.

Joseph: And look at all the wonderful work everyone in the neighborhood is bringing. I'm glad we have a place where we can all gather together to celebrate what we give to America.

Narrator: (Doorbell rings.) Many people came to Hull House for help.

Mary: We must work to get the country to agree to an eight-hour work day. Only then will everyone have enough time to take care of their families and stay healthy.

(The narrator rings the doorbell.)

Julia: Adults should earn enough so that their children don't have to work and can go to school.

Ellen: Jane, can we really do all that needs doing?

Jane: Why not? That's our job—to do anything it takes to make things better.

(The narrator rings the doorbell seven times in a row. Everyone is arranging themselves in a semicircle facing the audience. All together everyone applauds. In the middle of clapping they freeze and the narrator speaks.)

Narrator: Children in the neighborhood put on plays quite often at Hull House. Jane Addams helped to make costumes and direct scenes. Parents and friends attended the performances after work.

(The other characters unfreeze.)

Marie: What a lovely play!

Joseph: I wish there were more things like this for the children to do.

John: Yes, me too.

Jane: We've been talking to City Hall about the need for public spaces where children can play safely.

Ellen: They agreed to clear out an empty lot on the next block, and help create a ballfield where the children can play. They will build a jungle gym, too.

Jane: This way the children will get exercise in the fresh air.

Joseph: Will the city really go along with this plan?

Jane: Why not?

Narrator: And it did happen. Jane Addams started the country's first public playground in Chicago, because she set her mind to it and worked hard for it.

(The group applauds.)

In 1931, Jane Addams was awarded the Nobel Peace Prize. She donated her prize money of $16,000 plus $10,000 more of her own funds to it to the Women's International League of Peace and to Hull House.

(The group applauds, louder this time, and rises to give Jane Addams a standing ovation.)

THE END

~~~~~~~~~~~~~~~~~~~~~~~~~~~~~~~~~~~

Hull House served as a model for other settlement houses in the United States. At the settlement houses, people could learn English, receive care for their children, and get help in becoming American citizens. Many immigrants went on to start their own self-help organizations.

© Macmillan/McGraw-Hill

'Round the World with Nellie Bly

by Claire Daniel Chapelle

CAST:

Newsboy
Narrator
Mr. Goddard
Nellie Bly
Mr. Chambers
Passenger 1
Young Girl
Randolph Charles
Jules Verne
Madame Verne
Driver

Telegraph Operator
Irene Sarles
Mr. Sarles
Engineer
Ticket Agent
Mr. Fuhrmann
Japanese Reporter
Chief Allen
Passenger 2
John Jennings
Doctor

Newsboy: EXTRA! EXTRA! Read all about it! Get the latest edition of the *World* hot off the press!

Narrator: Back in the year 1888, people relied on newspapers to fill them in on all the news, for television and radio had not yet been invented. Almost every city had several competing newspapers, and nowhere was the competition more fierce than in New York City. *The Tribune,* the *Sun,* the *Times,* and the *World,* to name just a few of the papers, used every gimmick they could think of to attract readers. The *World,* a newspaper owned by Joseph Pulitzer, had the largest circulation of all, due in part to the articles of a talented young woman reporter named Nellie Bly. Nellie was always on the lookout for a sensational story idea to present to her editor, Mr. Goddard.

Mr. Goddard: Good morning, Nellie. Well, you look a little bleary-eyed this morning. Have you given any thought to this week's stories?

Nellie Bly: Morning, Mr. Goddard. I can imagine that I do look a little tired. You see, I stayed up all night doing nothing but thinking about possible stories, and I only managed to come up with one idea.

Mr. Goddard: You were up all night, and you only have one idea? Nellie, that doesn't sound like you!

Nellie Bly: Yes, but this idea isn't like most, Mr. Goddard. You see, I want to go around the world!

Mr. Goddard: Nellie, a trip around the world isn't a news story. People do that all the time.

Nellie Bly: The way I plan to do it will be a news story. I'll go around the world like Phileas Fogg, the hero in Jules Verne's book *Around the World in Eighty Days.* But the gimmick is that I'll beat Fogg's record and make the trip in seventy-five days! I know it'll work, Mr. Goddard. I stopped at a steamship office before coming to work this morning, and I've calculated that it will take me precisely 75 days and 4 hours!

Mr. Goddard: Well, Nellie, it's a good idea, but not a new one. I'm sorry to disappoint you, but the *World* has been kicking that notion around for quite a while. In fact, we got so far as deciding to send John Jennings.

Nellie Bly: Oh. . . . Well, Mr. Jennings is an excellent reporter, but just think how much more sensational it would be if a woman made the trip! We'd sell many more newspapers!

Mr. Goddard: I don't think there's anything I can do at this point, Nellie. You see, Mr. Chambers has already made the decision; but if you'd like, we can go talk to him.

Nellie Bly: Absolutely! Let's see him now! I'm sure he can be convinced to change his mind.

Mr. Goddard: Well, Nellie, if anyone can do it, you're the one!

Narrator: Mr. Goddard spoke from experience! You see, in 1888, few women worked outside the home, and for those who did, good jobs were hard to come by. Nellie Bly was one of the first female newspaper reporters, so she was used to hearing the opinion that a woman couldn't do what a man could. Determined to disprove that notion, Nellie Bly approached Julius Chambers, managing editor of the *World*, and described her idea.

Mr. Chambers: I don't think it's a good idea. I know you can do whatever you set your mind to, Nellie. But the fact that you're a woman complicates everything.

Nellie Bly: I've carried out much harder assignments, Mr. Chambers. Remember the time I disguised myself and worked side by side with the women in the box factory to expose dangerous working conditions?

Mr. Goddard: She's right, Chambers. And who could forget the ten days Nellie spent on Blackwell's Island posing as a mentally ill woman so she could report on conditions inside an insane asylum? Thanks to her articles, changes are being made.

Nellie Bly: And I've been in the most dangerous sections of New York and Pittsburgh. And travel isn't new to me; I went to Mexico . . .

Mr. Chambers: Accompanied by your mother . . .

Nellie Bly: But I had to take care of her!

Mr. Goddard: Nellie, even Jules Verne's hero Phileas Fogg was accompanied by a servant. You'd need a companion.

Nellie Bly: I'm not an Englishman who sits sipping tea while being waited on by servants. This is 1888, and I'm an American woman!

Mr. Chambers: Exactly my point! Women don't travel alone, American or not.

Nellie Bly: Now just a minute! When I investigated the mental health institute you let me go alone. I was hungry and cold and scared, but I survived to write about it. You owe me the chance to do this! And you know in your heart that I am the best person to go!

Mr. Chambers: But what about baggage? With all the belongings a woman has to take, it would slow you down. Besides, you don't speak any foreign languages. I know you're excited about the idea, but there's no point in discussing it further. Only a man could do this!

Nellie Bly: Very well. Send John Jennings if you want. I'll start the very same day for some other newspaper, and I'll beat him!

Mr. Chambers: Nellie, I believe you would.

Narrator: Both men looked at each other. It didn't take long for them to make up their minds.

Mr. Chambers: All right. If anyone goes, it will be you, Nellie. I promise.

Narrator: Almost a year passed without any more discussion of Nellie's idea. Then, one cold November evening, Mr. Chambers asked Nellie to step into his office.

Mr. Chambers: Can you be ready to start around the world the day after tomorrow?

Nellie Bly: I can start today!

Mr. Goddard: Nellie, we know you're resourceful, but how can you be ready so soon?

Nellie Bly: Phileas Fogg took an hour to pack, but I know I can beat his record! After all, I've had almost a year to plan!

Mr. Goddard: So, what will you take?

Nellie Bly: I'll take one small gripsack with a blouse, two caps, a blazer, and three veils to protect my face from the sun and wind. I'll also include pens and pencils, paper, pins, needles and thread, a dressing gown, slippers, toilet articles, underwear, handkerchiefs, and if I can fit it in, a jar of cold cream. I'll wear a two-piece dress and an overcoat and carry a silk raincoat.

Mr. Goddard: There, Chambers, what did I tell you? Do you still think her baggage will be a problem?

Narrator: On Thursday, November 14, 1889, Nellie arrived at the pier in Hoboken, New Jersey. The twenty-four-hour clock that would record her time was set, and Nellie boarded the steamship *Augusta Victoria*, At precisely 9:40 in the morning, the whistle blew and the steamship pulled away from the pier.

Newsboy: EXTRA! EXTRA! Read all about it! Nellie Bly to make an unequaled, rapid-transit, record-breaking trip around the globe! Read all about it in the latest edition of the *World*!

Narrator: On her way at last, Nellie leaned over the rail to wave at the crowd of well-wishers.

Nellie Bly: Good-bye! Don't worry! It's only a matter of 28,000 miles, and 75 days and 4 hours until I shall be back again! Think of me as having a wonderful vacation and the most enjoyable time of my life.

Passenger 1: My goodness, you've got quite a crowd to see you off!

Nellie Bly: Yes, I certainly do. In addition to my mother and a few friends, my editors and other business associates came down to the pier. You see, I'm attempting to beat Phileas Fogg's record and report on it for my paper, the *World*.

Passenger 1: Well, we certainly have a great day for sailing.

Nellie Bly: We do? As a matter of fact, the sea seems a bit choppy to me. Oooh! . . . Excuse me, I'm not feeling too well!

Passenger 1: Ha! And she thinks she's going around the world!

Narrator: Miserable with seasickness, Nellie went to her cabin and slept until 4:00 the next afternoon. When she awoke, she found that she had gotten her "sea legs," and every trace of seasickness was gone. It didn't take long for word to get around the ship about Nellie's trip. One young girl waited for an opportunity to talk with Nellie.

Young Girl: Ma'am, are you really going around the world?

Nellie Bly: Why, yes, I am.

Young Girl: I told my mother I wanted to go around the world, but she said girls don't do things like that.

Nellie Bly: She's right, usually they don't. But I'm trying to change people's attitudes, so we girls can do what we want to do.

Young Girl: I think you're a brave lady. I want to be like you when I grow up.

Narrator: Eight days later, on November 22nd, the *Augusta Victoria* docked in Southampton, England, at 2:30 in the morning. Despite the hour, Nellie was on deck with her gripsack in hand. She watched as a tall young man stepped off the tug that had nudged the ship into the pier.

Mr. Charles: Miss Bly? Miss Nellie Bly? I'm Randolph Charles, the London correspondent for the *World*. Is your baggage ready? Shall I call a porter.

Nellie Bly: This one bag is all I have, Mr. Charles.

Mr. Charles: It is? Then let's get you checked through customs. I've an important message for you from Monsieur and Madame Jules Verne. They've invited you to stop and see them.

Nellie Bly: The Vernes! How wonderful! I'd love to meet them, but it's not on my route. Is it possible to make a detour?

Mr. Charles: I think it can be done if you are willing to go without sleep for two days.

Nellie Bly: Sleep? I'd give up any amount of sleep to meet Jules Verne!

Mr. Charles: There is one other factor, Miss Bly. You must be clear about the risk. By changing your itinerary, you could ruin your schedule.

Nellie Bly: I think we should try it! I can't think of anyone I would like to meet more than Jules Verne! His character, Phileas Fogg, is the reason I'm here today. I think it's worth the risk; besides, my readers will love it! Think of all the newspapers we'll sell!

Narrator: So Nellie and Mr. Charles traveled by train to London and then to Dover. From there, they took a boat across the English Channel to France and caught a train to Amiens. Late that day, a tired but thrilled Nellie Bly arrived at the Vernes' beautiful estate. With Mr. Charles acting as translator, Nellie and the Vernes were able to carry on a conversation.

Jules Verne: Mademoiselle Bly, you are so young! You're almost a child!

Mme. Verne: But she is a remarkable young woman.

Nellie Bly: Thank you, madame. I would like to thank you for the kind invitation to visit your home.

Jules Verne: The pleasure is ours, dear lady. As a writer, I invent my characters. It's not often I meet someone such as you who has a life as interesting as a character in one of my books.

Mme. Verne: I'm curious, mademoiselle. How did you get the name Nellie Bly? It's not your real name, is it?

Nellie Bly: No, my real name is Elizabeth Cochrane, but American reporters often use pen names. After I finished my first news article, we were trying to think of a catchy name for me. Just then a reporter walked by humming an old Stephen Foster tune called "Nelly Bly," and I thought to myself, "That's the name for me! Nellie Bly!"

Mme. Verne: I admire you American women. You're so modern.

Nellie Bly: There's nothing so modern as your husband's novels. As one of your most avid readers,

Mr. Verne, there's something I've always been curious about. How did you get the idea for *Around the World in Eighty Days*?

Jules Verne: Well, Mademoiselle Bly, you'll be happy to learn that I got the idea from reading a newspaper. One morning I saw an article that said a journey around the world might be done in eighty days. Suddenly, a great idea for a story occurred to me! Suppose the main character was trying to prove that such a journey might be made. As you know, when we travel from west to east, we gain a day. Well, what would happen if the main character forgot all about the international dateline? He would think that he'd failed—only to find out at the last minute that he had succeeded after all! The idea worked, and the book turned out rather well. Now, tell me, how did you get the idea to try my idea?

Nellie Bly: About a year ago, I was up all night racking my brains for story ideas for my paper. When I couldn't think of anything new or different, I finally said to myself, "I might as well be halfway around the world!" Then I looked over at my bureau and saw your book. So I said to myself, "Why not? Why can't I do that?"

Jules Verne: And how do you plan to go?

Nellie Bly: I plan to follow Phileas Fogg's route most of the way. From here, I'll go to Calais on the French coast, and then on to Brindisi, Italy. From Italy, I'll travel to Port Said, Ismailia, and Suez, all in Egypt. Then I'll go to Aden in Yemen, then Colombo, Ceylon. My last stops will include Penang, the island of Singapore, the British colony of Hong Kong, and Yokohama in Japan. Finally, I'll sail to San Francisco and take a train across the United States back to New Jersey—all in less time than it took your hero, Mr. Verne!

Jules Verne: If you do it in seventy-nine days or less, I shall applaud you with both hands.

Mme. Verne: It is almost time for your train, my dear. We thank you very much for coming to see us.

Nellie Bly: Merci! Even if I don't complete the trip in time, it's been worth it just to meet you! Au revoir!

Narrator: The readers of the *World* seemed to think it was worth it, too, as they eagerly read Nellie's account.

Newsboy: EXTRA! EXTRA! Read all about it! Nellie Bly meets famous author Jules Verne! Only in today's *World*!

Narrator: From Amiens, Nellie Bly took the train to Calais. There she parted from Mr. Charles and caught yet another train for the two-day trip to Brindisi in southern Italy. On the train, Nellie wrote in her journal.

Narrator: The train arrived in Brindisi at 1:30 in the morning of the eleventh day of Nellie's trip. A large omnibus met the passengers and carried them down to the pier. Nellie found her cabin on the steamship Victoria, which was bound for Colombo, Ceylon. After stowing her bag, Nellie rushed back to the deck to find the omnibus driver.

Nellie Bly: Excuse me, sir, can you tell me if there is a telegraph office nearby? Would I have time to send a cable before we sail?

Driver: Yes, miss, there is a telegraph office that is not far from the pier. The streets are too narrow for my omnibus, but we can walk there. Since the ship is not due to sail for almost an hour, you can probably make it, if we hurry.

Nellie Bly: Hurrying is second nature to me. Let's go!

Narrator: The driver rushed Nellie down the gangplank and through several dark and winding streets.

Driver:	Ah, here we are!
Nellie Bly:	But the telegraph office is closed; there's no one here! My cable will have to wait until I reach the next port.
Driver:	Here it is customary to ring the night bell to awaken the operator. See, he's coming now. I'll translate for you, if you'd like.
Nellie Bly:	Thank you very much. Please tell him that I'm sorry to wake him, but I need to send a cable to New York.
Telegraph Operator:	New York? Where is that, young lady?
Nellie Bly:	Why, it's the biggest city in North America! Does he mean to say he's never heard of New York?
Telegraph Operator:	I've heard of York, England. Are you sure you have the name right? Perhaps you mean Yorkshire?
Nellie Bly:	No, indeed. I mean New York City in the state of New York in the United States of America.
Telegraph Operator:	One moment, please. I must find it first. Then I'll have to determine the cost. We don't send many cables to America. This will take some time.
Narrator:	The telegraph operator took out several large books and began to search through them for the information he needed.
Nellie Bly:	Please ask him to hurry! The boat leaves in fifteen minutes!
Telegraph Operator:	Ah, yes, here it is. New York, New York, in the United States. You were right, young lady! Do you have your message and the money? Good. I'll send this cable right away.
Narrator:	Just then a shrill whistle sounded.
Nellie Bly:	My ship! It's leaving without me!
Driver:	Can you run? Let's try to make it!

Narrator: Nellie Bly ran as fast as she could and reached the pier in time to see a steamship pulling away. But to her great relief, she discovered that it was another liner. Her ship, the *Victoria*, was still tied up! Meanwhile, back home, people eagerly reached for the newspapers to find out about Nellie Bly's progress.

Newsboy: EXTRA! EXTRA! Read all about it! Nellie Bly steams through the Suez Canal!

Narrator: Such was the topic of discussion at the breakfast table at the Sarles home in Rye, New York.

Irene Sarles: Has the *World* come today, Father? May I see it?

Mr. Sarles: Since when did you start to read the newspaper, young lady?

Irene Sarles: Since Nellie Bly started her trip around the world! She's been gone for twenty-four days. Haven't you been reading about it?

Mr. Sarles: I read the *New York Times*, not the *World*! So who, may I ask, is Nellie Bly?

Irene Sarles: Oh, Father! She's the woman who reports on conditions in factories and mental institutions for the World. Now she's trying to circle the globe in less time than Phileas Fogg.

Mr. Sarles: That's a foolish stunt! She'll never make it!

Irene Sarles: She's already made it across Europe and as far as Port Said. Now she's writing about her trip through the Suez Canal. Why, in this account, she describes how they dress for dinner and dine on board the ship, and how they spend their evenings on deck. She even tells about having dishwater poured on her one morning when her porthole was open!

Mr. Sarles: Goodness! That sounds positively dreadful!

Irene Sarles: But she makes everything seem so interesting! Do you know it's so hot at night that the men sleep on the deck? And listen to this! She describes the camel markets, Egyptian women in black veils, and boys diving from the banks of the canal for silver coins. According to her itinerary, she should be in Colombo, Ceylon, by now. Oh, what a trip!

Narrator: Nellie Bly was, indeed, in Colombo. And four days later, on December 12th, Nellie Bly was still in Colombo, cabling her reports back to New York and waiting impatiently for her ship to leave for China. Finally, the day of departure came, and Nellie boarded the *Oriental*. There she met the chief engineer strolling on the deck.

Engineer: Good morning! It's a lovely day for sailing, isn't it?

Nellie Bly: It will be when we set sail. Do you know when that will be?

Engineer: We can't sail until the *Nepaul* comes in. She was to have been here at daybreak, but she's a slow old boat.

Nellie Bly: But we're behind schedule! I've been waiting to leave for days!

Engineer: Well, at least Colombo is a pleasant place to visit. I hope you've had an opportunity to do some sightseeing. By any chance, did you ride in the rickshaws and visit the Buddhist temples and enjoy the wonderful Chinese food?

Nellie Bly: Yes, I did all that. But waiting is difficult for me. You see, I'm traveling around the world for my paper, and I'm trying to do it in seventy-five days. This is day twenty-nine, and I've got only forty-six more days to get back home!

Engineer: I see! Like Phileas Fogg! But since there's absolutely nothing you can do about the delay, you should try to relax and enjoy yourself.

Nellie Bly: I do apologize for seeming so out-of-sorts. I fear my patience has given out, due to the long delay. But you see, I have nightmares of creeping back to New York ten days behind schedule . . . a failure.

Narrator: At that precise moment, Nellie spotted a thin line of blue smoke just above the horizon.

Nellie Bly: Look! Do you see that smoke off in the distance? It looks like a steamship!

Engineer: I believe it's the *Nepaul*! As soon as she docks and her passengers are brought aboard, we'll sail.

Narrator: On December 16th, the *Oriental* anchored at Penang off the coast of Malaysia. Nellie Bly continued to cable her reports back to New York.

Mr. Chambers: What do we have from Nellie today, Goddard?

Mr. Goddard: It's good copy. She describes the Chinese places of worship in Penang where she drank tea with the priests. They couldn't say a word to each other, so they just smiled.

Mr. Chambers: It's hard to imagine Nellie not saying anything!

Mr. Goddard: Oh my goodness, just listen to this! She bought a monkey.

Mr. Chambers: A what?

Mr. Goddard: A monkey! In Singapore, she saw some monkeys and decided she had to have one, so she bought one. It's impossible to predict what Nellie will do next!

Mr. Chambers: Well, I know what we'll do. We'll print it. It'll make good copy—readers will love it! By the way, can't we think of something to get even more readers interested in Nellie?

Mr. Goddard: How about a contest of some sort? . . . Yes! A contest to predict when Nellie will make it back.

Mr. Chambers: Brilliant! It'll get all New York involved! Everyone will want to keep track of Nellie's journey, and the only way they'll be able to do that is by reading the *World*!

Newsboy: EXTRA! EXTRA! Read all about it! Enter the Nellie Bly Guessing Match! Get your coupon in this issue of the *World*!

Narrator: Meanwhile, on the way from Singapore to Hong Kong, Nellie's ship encountered a monsoon. Rains fell and wild winds rocked the boat. Nellie's cramped cabin was flooded. Despite the monsoon, Nellie reached Hong Kong on the morning of December 23rd—two days early! She immediately made her way to a ticket office and eagerly approached the agent.

Nellie Bly: Good morning. Can you please tell me the date of the first sailing for Japan?

Ticket Agent: Excuse me, but are you Nellie Bly? We've been looking for a woman by that name traveling alone from Singapore.

Nellie Bly: Why, yes, I'm Nellie Bly. You must have heard about my trip. I'm ahead of schedule! Isn't that wonderful?

Ticket Agent: Miss Bly, I'm afraid I have bad news for you. You're going to be beaten.

Nellie Bly: How can that be? I've made up for the five days I lost in Colombo, unless . . . unless the boat to Japan has sunk!

Ticket Agent: The steamship hasn't sunk, but you are going to lose.

Nellie Bly: Lose? I don't understand. What do you mean?

Ticket Agent: Aren't you having a race around the world?

Nellie Bly: Of course! I'm running a race with time!

Ticket Agent: Time? I don't think that's her name. The other woman . . .

Nellie Bly: Her name? The other woman? What are you talking about?

Ticket Agent: Don't you know? The day you left New York, another woman named Elizabeth Bisland started out in the opposite direction. She's trying to beat you, and it looks as if she's going to do it. She has thousands of dollars to pay ships to leave early. Do you have that kind of money?

Nellie Bly: No, of course not!

Ticket Agent: Well, she left here three days ago. Based on the scheduled sailing dates, you can't even leave Hong Kong for at least five days. And then you'll have to wait five more days in Yokohama.

Nellie Bly: So it's impossible to catch up?

Ticket Agent: I'm afraid so. I must say, I'm astonished you didn't know about her. I was told that your paper sent her.

Nellie Bly: That's impossible! Mr. Chambers would never do such a thing!

Narrator: As Nellie and the ticket agent were speaking, a ship's officer approached the window. He was from the *Oceanic*, the ship scheduled to take Nellie to Japan and then on to San Francisco.

Mr. Fuhrmann: So you're our famous passenger Nellie Bly. It's a pleasure to meet you! I recognized you from the cartoons that I saw in the newspapers we picked up in San Francisco. I couldn't help overhearing part of your conversation, and I want to say that you shouldn't worry about someone beating you around the world. This other woman is just trying to steal your idea for her magazine, the *Cosmopolitan*. Your newspaper didn't send her to race against you.

Nellie Bly: I knew they'd never do that! You see, I promised my editor I'd go around the world in seventy-five days, and that's what I'll do. I'm not racing with anybody—except Phileas Fogg!

Mr. Fuhrmann: That's the spirit!

Narrator: While waiting for the ship to Japan, Nellie Bly explored Hong Kong. After climbing a mountain high above the city, she wrote this entry in her journal on December 24, 1889.

Nellie Bly: "The view is superb. The bay . . . lies calm and serene, dotted with hundreds of ships that seem like tiny toys. The palatial white houses come halfway up the mountain side, beginning at the edge of the glassy bay. . . . One seems to be suspended between two heavens. Every one of the several thousand boats and sampans carries a light after dark. This, with the lights on the roads and in the houses, seems to be a sky more filled with stars than the one above."

Narrator: Meanwhile, back in New York, readers eagerly awaited each edition of the *World* to track Nellie Bly's progress.

Newsboy: EXTRA! EXTRA! Read all about it. Nellie Bly now in Japan. World-famous globe-trotter has reached Yokohama!

Irene Sarles: Father, did you bring home today's edition of the *World*? I'm dying to read about Nellie Bly!

Mr. Sarles: Nellie Bly, Nellie Bly! That's all I hear around this house!

Irene Sarles: Father, listen to Nellie's latest report from Yokohama; it's dated January 3rd. She says, "I arrived here today safely and in good health . . . . The commander of the *Oceanic* expects to make an extraordinary effort between here and San Francisco . . . . I hope to be in New York January 25. Happy New Year to all my friends in America." Father, I think she's going to make it!

Mr. Sarles: I hope she does. But she's still got a long way to go.

Irene Sarles: There's a coupon for a contest in the newspaper. All you have to do is predict exactly how long you think it will take Nellie to complete her trip. I'm going to cut it out and send it in!

Mr. Sarles: Those newspaper editors will do anything to get you to buy their papers.

Irene Sarles: Oh, come on, Father! The winner gets a free trip to Europe and $250 spending money! You can enter, too! I'll save you the coupon in tomorrow's paper. I predict she'll make it in exactly 72 days, 7 hours, and 4 minutes! What do you think?

Mr. Sarles: I think I'd like to see that newspaper after you've finished reading it.

Narrator: While Nellie was in Japan, a reporter from a Japanese newspaper interviewed her about her visit.

Reporter: Did you enjoy Japan, Miss Bly?

Nellie Bly: Oh yes! If I were married, I would tell my husband I know where Eden is, and I would bring him to Japan. Japan is beautiful. Your cities are clean, and your people are full of grace and charm.

Reporter: What has been the most unusual thing you have seen?

Nellie Bly: Everything is unusual. In fact, in a place like this, it's unusual for anything to be familiar! It's all strange—and quite wonderful. For example, you dress so differently! A Japanese woman wears a flowing kimono with long sleeves in which she carries her calling cards, money, combs, and hairpins. And your houses, with their sliding doors and rice-paper windows instead of glass, are nothing like the houses in America. Everything here enchants me.

Reporter: Is there anything you would do differently if you could begin your trip all over again?

Nellie Bly: Yes, I would bring along one of those new cameras made by George Kodak. I want to remember all that I've seen, and it would have been nice to have pictures.

Narrator: Two days later, on January 7th, Nellie boarded the *Oceanic* to sail to San Francisco. The ship's engineer, Chief Allen, had prepared a surprise for her.

Chief Allen: Welcome, Miss Bly! In honor of your trip, we've posted this motto above the engines. It says, "For Nellie Bly, we'll win or die."

Nellie Bly: That's wonderful, Chief Allen! I have precisely twenty-one days left. Full steam ahead!

Narrator: In the New York offices of the *World*, Nellie's editors were busy planning.

Mr. Chambers: Goddard, here are the designs for our new Nellie Bly parlor game. We'll call it "Round the World with Nellie Bly."

Mr. Goddard: Great! We'll run it right after she gets back.

Mr. Chambers: By the way, I just received a cable saying that Nellie has left Japan. What plans have we made for her welcome in San Francisco?

Mr. Goddard: The mayor and the press club will meet her ship. As she steps ashore, a band will play "Home Sweet Home" and "Nelly Bly."

Mr. Chambers: Shouldn't someone from the New York office be there, too? How about Jennings?

Mr. Goddard: Good idea. Since he didn't get to make the trip around the world, the least we can do is send him to accompany Nellie on her special train home.

Narrator: However, out on the Pacific Ocean, the weather wasn't cooperating with Nellie's schedule. On January 9th, her third day out from Japan, a

monsoon hit. The ship pitched violently in the rolling seas. News of the storm reached the New York offices of the *World* and made the headlines.

Newsboy: EXTRA! EXTRA! Read all about it! Will Nellie Bly survive a fierce monsoon?

Nellie Bly: Chief Allen, I only have nineteen days left! With this storm, I don't think I'll make it back in time. If I fail, I'll be too ashamed to go back to New York.

Chief Allen: Don't talk that way, Miss Bly. We're doing everything we can. I'm running the engines harder than they've ever been run before, and the entire crew is pitching in. So, chin up and smile, Miss Bly. We're doing our very best!

Narrator: Unknown to Nellie, another storm in another part of the world was also threatening her trip. A blizzard, raging in the western part of the United States, was burying the rails on the transcontinental route that Nellie was to take home. Stuck in a snowdrift, someplace in the Sierra Nevada Mountains, was the train carrying reporter John Jennings, Nellie's escort home.

Passenger 2: Jennings, we've been snowbound here for hours. Do you have any idea where we are?

Mr. Jennings: Well, sir, I was just talking with the conductor. He says this place is called Emigrant Gap. There must be ten feet of snow on the tracks already, and it's still coming down in flakes the size of soda crackers!

Passenger 2: Did the conductor say how they plan to get us out of here?

Mr. Jennings: This train can't move until the rotary snowplows get here, but that could take days.

Narrator: And it did. It was several days before word of Jennings's plight reached the New York office of the *World*.

Mr. Goddard: Chambers, read this! It's a telegram from Jennings. He's snowbound in that blizzard.

Mr. Chambers: Let's see. . . . He says they've been stuck for fifty hours. The snow is twelve to eighteen feet deep in places, and some miners on snowshoes have brought food to the passengers. That's quite a story right there—print it!

Mr. Goddard: Right away, boss! By the way, we're busy rerouting Nellie's special train for the trip back. It's clear she won't be able to travel across the country on the northern route as we'd planned.

Narrator: Back at sea, the monsoon finally blew itself out, and the ship reached San Francisco on January 21st.

Newsboy: EXTRA! EXTRA! Read all about it! Nellie Bly's ship sighted in San Francisco harbor on day sixty-eight of her historic trip!

Narrator: With just seven days remaining, what could go wrong now?

Mr. Fuhrmann: Attention all passengers! I regret to announce that the ship's doctor is unable to locate our health certificate. We fear it may have been left back in Yokohama. If that is the case, no one will be permitted to land until the next ship arrives from Japan!

Nellie Bly: Then I'll just have to jump overboard and swim ashore!

Narrator: At that moment, the ship's doctor came running in.

Doctor: Fortunately, that won't be necessary, Miss Bly. I found the certificate stuck in a cubbyhole in my desk! Unfortunately, however, there is a report that we have a case of smallpox on board; everyone will have to be examined.

Nellie Bly: How long will that take?

Mr. Fuhrmann: Don't worry, Miss Bly. I've asked the doctor to examine you first.

Narrator: Following a quick examination, Nellie boarded a waiting tugboat that was to take her into the San Francisco harbor. As the tugboat steamed away, the doctor leaned over the ship's railing and called out.

Doctor: Miss Bly! Wait! Stop! I forgot to examine your tongue! You cannot land until I see it!

Nellie Bly: All right! How's this, Doctor?

Narrator: With that, Nellie Bly stuck out her tongue at the doctor.

Doctor: Looks fine to me!

Narrator: After a rousing welcome home to America, Nellie's special train left San Francisco. Two hours later, the train stopped in Lathrop, California, to pick up another passenger—John Jennings.

Nellie Bly: Mr. Jennings, what a surprise! A *World* reporter in San Francisco told me that you were trapped in a snowbound train someplace in the Sierra Nevada Mountains! How on earth did you get here, and are you all right?

Mr. Jennings: I'm fine now, thanks, but I had to hike fourteen miles on snowshoes to get to a train that would bring me here.

Nellie Bly: Fourteen miles through snowdrifts! How did you find your way?

Mr. Jennings: One of the miners served as my guide. In fact, it was his wife's snowshoes that I wore.

Nellie Bly: You've done a brave thing. I can see why Mr. Chambers wanted to send you around the world.

Mr. Jennings: And yet you, Miss Bly, were an even better choice. It looks like you'll make it in time.

Nellie Bly: I haven't made it yet. Have you heard anything about the other woman—Elizabeth Bisland?

Mr. Jennings: Not a word. She's probably in the middle of the Atlantic Ocean right now. Don't worry; you're going to make it.

Narrator: From there, the special train carrying Nellie Bly sped across the United States, stopping along the way so that people could see and talk to the remarkable woman. Nellie passed through Chicago and Philadelphia, and then, on January 25th—the seventy-second day of her journey—she arrived at her final destination—Jersey City.

All Except Nellie Bly: Hurrah! Hurrah for Nellie Bly!

Narrator: The cannons in New York Harbor boomed out the news of Nellie's arrival. She took off her cap, threw it into the crowd, and then addressed her well-wishers.

Nellie Bly: I'm so happy, and not only because I've gone around the world in seventy-two days, but because I'm home!

Narrator: Nellie Bly had beaten Phileas Fogg's time by nearly eight days! When the official watch was checked, 72 days, 6 hours, 11 minutes, and 14 seconds had elapsed. Elizabeth Bisland, the young woman who had tried to challenge Nellie, did not arrive until four days later. Not only had Nellie done what she set out to do, she'd also established a record that would stand for thirty-nine years. More important, she had shown the world what a determined young woman could do!

Think-Aloud
COPYING MASTERS

I wonder . . .

Think-Aloud Copying Master 1

I made a connection when . . .

I was able
to picture
in my mind . . .

I figured out _____ because . . .

I thought _____ was important in this text because . . .

When I read _____,
I had to re-read,
read back, read on . . .

LITERATURE INDEX by GENRE

Biography and Autobiography

Fiction

Realistic Fiction

Science Fiction

Folk Tales, Tall Tales, and Fables

Nonfiction

Informational Nonfiction

Primary Sources

Plays and Choral Readings

Poetry

ACKNOWLEDGMENTS ———————— Continued

Excerpt from MOJAVE by Diane Siebert. Copyright © 1998 by Diane Siebert. Used by permission of HarperCollins Publishers.

Excerpt from ROBOTS RISING by Carol Sonenklar. Copyright © 1999 by Carol Sonenklar. Used by permission of Henry Holt and Company, LLC.

"The Mother of the Movement" from REMEMBER THE BRIDGE: POEMS OF A PEOPLE by Carole Boston Weatherford. Copyright © 2002 by Carole Boston Weatherford. Used by permission of Philomel Books.

"Ptooey!" by Lisa Schneider from *Ranger Rick*, August 2003. Copyright © 2003 by National Wildlife Federation. Used by permission of National Wildlife Federation.

"Nature's Fury: For Better or Worse" by Stephen James O'Meara from *Odyssey*, February 2005. Copyright © 2004 by Carus Publishing Company. Used by permission of Carus Publishing Company.

"The Hen and the Apple Tree" from FABLES by Arnold Lobel. Copyright © 1980 by Arnold Lobel. Used by permission of Scholastic Inc.

"The Circle and the Poles" from A WORLD OF WONDERS: GEOGRAPHIC TRAVELS IN VERSE AND RHYME by J. Patrick Lewis. Copyright © 2002 by J. Patrick Lewis. Used by permission of Dial Books for Young Readers, a division of Penguin Putnam Inc.

"Looking Back at Vegetables" from LOOKING BACK AT FOOD AND DRINK by Anne Mountfield. Copyright © 1988 by Schoolhouse Press, Inc. Used by permission of Schoolhouse Press, Inc.

"All But Blind" from SOUNDS OF MYSTERY by Bill Martin Jr. with Peggy Brogan and John Archambault. Copyright © 1991 by DLM. Used by permission of The Literary Trustees of Walter de la Mare and The Society of Authors as their representative.

Excerpt from TOP SECRET: A HANDBOOK OF CODES, CIPHERS, AND SECRET WRITING by Paul B. Janeczko. Copyright © 2004 by Paul B. Janeczko. Used by permission of Candlewick Press.

"Yeh-hsien" from THE ORYX MULTICULTURAL FOLKTALE SERIES: CINDERELLA by Judy Sierra. © 1992 Oryx Press, Phoenix, AZ.

"John Muir: Man of the Mountains (1838–1914)" by Ginger Wadsworth from *California Chronicles*, January 2000. Copyright © 2000 by Cobblestone Publishing Company. Used by permission of Cobblestone Publishing Company.

"The Seeing Stick" by Jane Yolen. Copyright © 1977 by Jane Yolen. Reprinted by permission of HarperCollins Publishers.

"The Montgolfier Brothers" from FEATHERS, FLAPS, & FLOPS: FABULOUS EARLY FLIERS by Bo Zaunders. Copyright © 2001 by Bo Zaunders. Used by permission of Dutton Children's Books.

"The Microscope" by Maxine Kumin from THE POET'S TALES: A NEW BOOK OF STORY POEMS selected by William Cole. Copyright © 1971 by The World Publishing Company. Used by permission of The World Publishing Company.

Cover Illustrations: Donna Perrone

Illustrators Credits: Dan Krovatin, 17–22, 92–97; Madeline Sorel, 23–25; Kelly Murphy, 26–32, 85–88; Joel Iskowitz, 33–38, 146; Mike Biegel, 39–42; Eva Cockrille, 43–47; Hugh Harrison, 48–51, 82–84, 147–155; Paula Wendland, 52–54; Sandy Rabinowitz, 55–59; Laurie Harden, 60–63, 156–173; Janet Montecalvo, 64–68; Amanda Harvey, 69–72; Donna Perrone, 73–77; Ashley Mims, 78–81, 141–143; Susan Spellman, 89–91; David Erickson, 98–100; Gerardo Suzan, 101–103; Stephen Marchesi, 104–107, 199–206; Pam Carroll, 108–110 ; Doug Panton, 111–114; Gerry O'Neill, 115–119; Barbara Pollack, 120–123; Roman Dunets, 124–126; Chi Chung, 127–135; Brian Lies, 136–140; Janet Hamlin, 174–198; Gioia Fiammenghi, 207–230